CATALAN
COOKING

A DELICIOUS JOURNEY
THROUGH THE THOUSAND FLAVOURS
OF AN UNFORGETTABLE LAND

BONECHI

HOW TO READ THE CHARTS

DIFFICULTY	FLAVOUR	NUTRITIONAL VALUE
● Easy	● Mild	● Low
●● Quite easy	●● Tasty	●● Medium
●●● Difficult	●●● Spicy	●●● High

Project: Casa Editrice Bonechi
Series editor: Alberto Andreini
Concept and coordination: Paolo Piazzesi
Graphic design: Andrea Agnorelli and Maria Rosanna Malagrinò
Cover: Andrea Agnorelli
Make-up: Vanni Berti
Editing: Patrizia Chirichigno

Translation: Shona C. Dryburgh

Chef: Lisa Mugnai
Dietician: Dr. John Luke Hili

*The photographs relative to the recipes are property of the Casa Editrice Bonechi
photographic archives and were taken by* Andrea Fantauzzo.

*The other photographs used in this publication are property of the Casa Editrice Bonechi
photographic archives and were taken by*
Marco Bonechi, Luigi Di Giovine, Paolo Giambone, Andrea Pistolesi, Alessandro Saragosa.

© Copyright 2005
by CASA EDITRICE BONECHI, Firenze - Italia
E-mail: bonechi@bonechi.it   Internet: www.bonechi.it   www.bonechi.com

Printed in Italy by Centro Stampa Editoriale Bonechi.

The cover, layout and artworks by the Casa Editrice Bonechi *graphic artists in this publication,
are protected by international copyright.*

ISBN 88-476-1254-3

***

THE LAND OF IMPLANTED FLAVOURS

In Catalonia, *alioli* sauce is made the same as in Provence and in Languedoc, spaghetti are used like in Naples and cannelloni as in Bologna; all the same, this is not to be looked upon as 'borrowed' cooking or, worse still, as the adoption of cuisine from other countries due to a lack of personal resources or imagination. On the contrary, these and other examples represent the creative outcome of continuous progression in Catalonian cookery, of shoots inexhaustibly grafted on to its boughs to yield fresh blooms; this is the land that has taken the *paella*, which originated in Valencia, only to invent its own *paella parellada* and the irresistible *fideua*, a variation of *paella* made with pasta instead of rice. As we shall see on our tasty journey through the flavours of Catalonia, the cookery in this area is so used to mixing elaborate dishes with simple, family fare that it can consequently offer high-class preparations and traditional family cooking with the same elegance and flair, often associating the two fundamental properties of the Catalan landscape: the sea and the mountains. The Catalan table is both sophisticated and basic, elegant yet humble, and its dishes are a harmonious, enjoyable blend of sweet and savoury; chocolate is a recurrent ingredient, like in the *estofat de bou*, for example, and then there are very simple preparations such as the ever-present *pan amb tomaquet*, which foresees slices of farmhouse bread rubbed all over with garlic and tomatoes. Over the years, Catalonia has refined its culinary skill to the highest of standards, and its cookery is based on four mainstays: *picada*, *romesco*, *samfaina* and *sofrito*, sauces that are not

merely condiments or accompaniments but are, in line with the dictates of the finest of international cuisine, the foundations over which its dishes are constructed. Confirmation of the Catalan tendency to synthesise can be seen in its capability to produce dishes that are difficult to classify against normal standards of service (hors d'œuvres, first course, second course, or *entrée* and *plat*, etc) and which appear to belong to all categories, or to none of them at all, like the various rice dishes (*arros a banda, arroz a la catalana, arroz con habas*, and so on and so forth), which in effect are all in one courses like the pasta dishes (*fideos a la catalana, fideos con mariscos*, and the already mentioned *fideua*) or those with vegetables (*berenjenas, coles* and *espinacas a la catalana*), among which we find the famous *habas a la catalana*, made with lard, *butifarra* and a multitude of aromatic herbs.

Even the salads are so versatile that they can be served as accompaniments, light meals or even as hors d'œuvres when presented elegantly: both *amanida* and *xato* are fine examples of accompaniments whereas the excellent *esqueixada de bacalao* can be served as light meal, and *escalivada* can become an hors d'œuvres. As far as desserts and pastries are concerned, top place must be given to the famous *crema catalana*, closely followed by the delicate *menjar blanc* or the simple and nutritious *mel i mató*, then come *postre de músic* and a host of other delicacies.

Traditional and modern cooking trends live hand in hand in Catalonia without clashing. In Barcelona, which has hosted some of the

most famous restaurants in Europe since the beginning of the twentieth century, one can find an enormous variety of cooking styles, from Catalan to that of all the other Spanish regions, from that enjoyed in all Mediterranean lands to dishes from all over Europe and the world. Nevertheless, the crowning glory of all the recipes is definitely the time-honoured *escudella i carn d'olla*, the famous Catalan version (and never has a version been so delicious!) of the Spanish *cocido*: here we have soup, a second course and accompaniment, all in the same pot. In the Gerona region, the area that lies between the Pyrenees and Costa Brava and famous not only for its meats but also for the types of fish that make up the delicious *suquet de pescado*, the cookery is typical of many border areas: a blend of flavours, sweet mixed with savoury, or fusions of meat and fish, like in the various *mar i terra* dishes in which chicken and lobster happily combine (*langosta a la Costa Brava* is an unsurpassed example) or pork and mussels in the similar *porc amb musclos*. Much the same happens in the inland areas, where rabbit and snails are found together in *conejo con caracoles* and where

Barcelona: the fairy tale pinnacles of the **Sagrada Família,** *Antonio Gaudí's masterpiece.*
Above: *a panoramic view of the city and,* **previous page,** *Plaça Portal de a Pau.*

snails are cooked in many other ways (*caracoles a la patarrallada, caracoles "a la llauna"*). In this area, well known for its game (*perdices con coles*) and, above all for its exquisite fowl, the apex is definitely its special Christmas dish: *pavo relleno a la catalana*. In the Lérida area, which is renowned for a variety of cured meats such as *xolis* sausages, *girella* or *confitat*, similar to the French *confit* made with goose but made here with pork preserved under lard, the flavours are distinctive and the dishes are simple, with an abundance of rice and game. Tarragona, the ancient Roman capital of *Tarraconensis Hispania,* not far from the Ebro estuary, can tempt us with typical coastline fare like *gambas en salsa "romesco"* or a delicious *arros negre* or even *pataco,* tuna fish with mussels and vegetables, but also with dishes made in its countryside, like the tasty *conejo al estilo tarraconense.*

We cannot finish off without a tribute to the famous Catalan wines from the vineyards in Ampurdán, Alella, Penedès, Priorat and Costers del Segre. Wine has always been drunk in these areas and the people here are so used to the Bacchus nectar that instead of drinking it from normal glasses, they pour it directly down their throats from the typical *porrón*, a container shaped like a watering-can with a long spout, out of which the liquid flows into the mouth of the skilful drinker. The ones considered the most significant of these wines, even in past times, are those from Priorat, an area behind Tarragona where the earth is rocky and rich in slate; these vines, which were first introduced by the Romans, then cultivated on a series of natural and artificial terraces during the Middle Ages by the monks who inhabited the many monasteries erected here and there, yield robust, 14-20° grade wines with distinctive 'mineral' overtones, thanks to the mild to cool climate. Besides the red wines (which rate amongst the best in the world) there are also white (straw coloured wines with an intense fruity bouquet and a hint of mountain herbs), rosé and dessert wines. A little farther North, between Tarragona and Barcelona, we come to Penedès where wines are produced in vineyards caressed by the sea breezes that whisper upwards towards the imposing fortifications of Monserrat. This is another area where the labour of ancient Romans followed by the toils of Benedictine and Cistercian monks have created wines since historical times. The white wines that stand out here are young, refreshing and lively and the red ones are noble, often matured in *barriques*, but they are all a perfect complement to any high-standard cooking, like that in Catalonia. And what can we finish off with? A

toast to your health, of course, with a goblet of sparkling San Sadurni d'Anoia *cava* which, once tasted, will not allow you to yearn for French champagne.

A few explanations

Most of the recipes given here, especially those that require a certain amount of attention during their preparation, are illustrated with a series of step-by-step photographs to help the cook. We suggest you read the list of ingredients carefully (as

The unusual Teatre-Museu Dalí in Figueres. Above: Barcelona, Casa Batlló designed by A. Gaudí.

well as the charts, which indicate how long it will take to prepare and cook the dishes, their difficulty, the strength of their flavour, their nutritional value), then every step of the method, all before attempting it. Then, of course – *bon appetit*!

A technical detail: where 'ground pimiento' is mentioned, whether in the list of ingredients or in the text of the method, this has been indicated as *pimentón*, a spice (not necessarily very hot) obtained from dried and ground *capsicum annuum*, fiery red in colour and strong in flavour. The type found in Catalonia is either *fuerte* (hot) or *dulce* (mild) and the choice depends upon personal taste and eating habit. This ground pimiento is an actual ingredient, necessary for the success of the recipe and not just an 'artistic touch' added to make the dishes more appetising.

Some English speaking countries erroneously translate this ingredient with the word *paprika*, but this is not to be confused with Hungarian paprika, which is obtained from an Indian variety of small peppers with smaller pods and a more pungent fragrance; the *pimentón* spice is made from varieties that were brought over from the New World. Though paprika is different regards flavour, colour and gastronomic value, either its hot or mild strengths may be used instead of *pimentón*, or even the ground pimiento found in shops that sell biological produce. Other explanations regarding typical Catalan ingredients or products, like the famous *butifarra*, are given below the recipes that require them.

A FEW WORDS FROM THE DIETICIAN

*E*ating habits in Catalonia are definitely to be considered belonging to the so-called Mediterranean diet. In fact, we can see that the all-in-one dishes, so typical of Spain, are here skilful combinations of rice, or of pasta made from hard wheat-flour (*fideua* and *fideos*), and consequently rich in the complex carbohydrates or starches contained in these cereals (the principal daily intake is a 55-60% prevalence of sugars, therefore), vegetables (raw or cooked, giving 20-25 g of fibre per day, especially the so-called 'insoluble' fibres), extra virgin olive oil (the main, almost sole intake of lipids in the Mediterranean diet, particularly oleic acid which is beneficial for the arteries and the heart), a prevalence of white meat (in particular, rabbit and chicken, which are rich in polyunsaturated fats, other fatty acids that also exert beneficial properties on the circulation) and, of course, fish (especially the species caught locally off the coast). Daily protein intake is moderate, around 15%, whereas spicy sauces are frequently found, a custom left over from ancient days when spices were used to prevent food deteriorating (spices have always been considered excellent preservatives and condiments and are found all around the Mediterranean basin). Lastly, as in all the areas of this region, the traditional dishes prepared along the coast differ from those enjoyed inland but, apart from the difference in the ingredients called for, Catalan cooking is invariably part of the Mediterranean diet.

TABLE OF CONTENTS

Barcelona: the entrance staircase to the Hundred-Column Chamber, in Parc Güell.

4: Fish, shellfish and seafood

5: Eggs and vegetables

6: Cakes and desserts

Tourist harbours and modern facilities along the Costa Brava.

APPETISERS AND SNACKS

*All the tempting snacks
and titbits offered in the famous
tapa bar in Barcelona, starting with the celebrated
patatas bravas; tiny savoury pastries,
delicately flavoured salads, irresistible shrimps,
to be enjoyed one after the other,
delicacies to work up your appetite
while you talk with your friends.*

1

AMANIDA

Catalan salad ▶

1 head of curly endive
2 ribs of celery
2 spring onions
2 eggs
Butifarra (see page 22),
   100 g (4 oz) in one piece
Lean raw cured ham,
   50 g (2 oz) in one piece
2-3 salted (or in oil)
   anchovies
Alioli (see recipe for *Suquet de pescado* on page 73)
Vinegar
Salt

Serves: 6-8	
Preparation: 20'	
Cooking: 10'	
Difficulty: ●	
Flavour: ● ●	
Kcal (per serving): 188	
Proteins (per serving): 7	
Fats (per serving): 16	
Nutritional value: ● ●	

Put the eggs in a small pot, cover them with cold water, bring to the boil and hard boil for 7 minutes; leave to cool for a few minutes then shell them. Rinse the salt off the anchovies under cold running water (or drain them if under oil), fillet them, remove the heads and bones then leave to one side. Rinse and trim the vegetables according to their use. Tear the endive leaves into bite-size pieces and put them in a salad bowl together with the onions sliced into rings, the celery cut into fine strips and the diced ham. Season with a pinch of salt, a few drops of vinegar and mix. Chop the anchovy fillets and crumble the *butifarra* before adding them both to the salad. Garnish with slices of hard-boiled egg and serve accompanied by *alioli* in a sauce-boat. Each guest will help himself to the salad and dress it with this appetising garlic mayonnaise.

This salad is not only excellent when served as hors d'œuvres or along with other tapas but if the doses are increased proportionately it will become an enjoyable summer meal.

PAN AMB TOMAQUET

Bread and tomato appetisers

4 large slices of slightly stale
   farmhouse bread
2 ripe fleshy tomatoes
4 cloves of garlic
Salt and pepper
Olive oil

Serves: 4	
Preparation: 10'	
Difficulty: ●	
Flavour: ● ● ●	
Kcal (per serving): 267	
Proteins (per serving): 5	
Fats (per serving): 11	
Nutritional value: ● ●	

Peel the cloves of garlic and rub them over both sides of the slices of bread. Rinse the tomatoes and cut them in half to remove their seeds; rub each half tomato over one side of the bread slices until all the tomato flesh and juice has been used up. Sprinkle a little salt and a drizzle of oil over the bread slices then cut them into quarters: the result is a simple but very tasty appetiser, though it can be served as a delicious snack at any time of the day, as long as the oil is high quality and the tomatoes are fleshy. Some people prefer to add slices of raw cured ham, or even the exquisite anchovies from Cadaqués or Escala on the Roses Gulf that used to be eaten for breakfast.

COQUETES CON SAMFAINA

Vegetable pastries

Tinned tuna fish,
    120 g (5 oz)
Green and black olives
    in brine
Pickled caper berries
Salt and pepper
Olive oil

For the pastry
Plain flour, 400 g
    (14 oz; 3 ³/4 cups)
Baker's yeast, 20 g
    (³/4 oz; 1 ¹/2 tbsp)

For the samfaina
1 aubergine
1 green sweet pepper
1 gourgette
Half an onion
2 cloves of garlic
2 ripe cooking tomatoes

Serves: 8	
Preparation: 25'+2h	
Cooking: 40'	
Difficulty: ●●●	
Flavour: ●●●	
Kcal (per serving): 378	
Proteins (per serving): 11	
Fats (per serving): 17	
Nutritional value: ●●●	

1 Put the flour and a pinch of salt into a large baking bowl and mix; dissolve the yeast in a little lukewarm water, make a well in the flour and pour the yeast into the middle of it. Mix everything together (by hand or with a hand-mixer), adding 2-3 tablespoons of oil and enough water to obtain a smooth, stiff dough; work the dough into a ball then cover it with a clean kitchen cloth and leave it to stand for 2 hours.

2 In the meantime, half an hour before starting to prepare the *samfaina*, put the peeled and sliced aubergine on a platter, cover it with salt then weigh it down with some heavy object so that all the bitterness will 'sweat out'. When it is time to make the *samfaina*, rinse and trim the pepper, tomatoes and gourgette; rinse the salt off the slices of aubergine, pat them dry with kitchen paper then cut them into small cubes.

3 Peel the garlic, finely slice the half onion and cut the pepper into strips; sauté them all together in a pot (preferably earthenware) with 4-5 tablespoons of oil. Add the cubed aubergine and a pinch each of salt and pepper. After 5-6 minutes, add the tomatoes cut into pieces and the gourgette sliced into rounds; put a lid on the pot, lower the heat and allow to simmer very gently; after 15 minutes, take the lid off the pot and allow the liquid to reduce.

4 Using a rolling pin, roll out the pastry to 3-4 mm (¹/8 inch) thick; with a pastry cutter, or a drinking glass, cut out about twenty rounds of pastry 10 cm (4 inches) in diameter. Spread spoonfuls of *samfaina* over the pastry rounds then put them on a metal baking tin greased with oil. Bake in the oven, preheated to 200°C (375-400°F), for about 20 minutes. Cut the drained tuna fish into small pieces and use it, as well as the olives and capers, to garnish the *coquetes* when ready. Serve them hot along with other *tapas*.

GAMBAS EN SALSA *ROMESCO*

Prawns in a spicy sauce dip

1 Blanch the prawn tails for 5-6 minutes in slightly salted boiling water; drain, arrange them on a serving dish and garnish with sprigs of parsley. Place toothpicks in a holder near the dish so guests can spear the prawns before dipping them into the sauce.

2 Rinse, trim and prepare all the vegetables according to their use. Toast the almond and hazelnut kernels in a 160°C (320°F) oven for about 10 minutes; allow them to cool slightly then peel them. Toss fry the dried peppers in a pan with 5-6 tablespoons of oil; remove with a draining spoon and leave to dry on kitchen paper. Fry the almonds and hazelnuts in the oil left in the pan, remove and drain on kitchen paper. Lastly, still using the same oil, fry the crumbled bread and drain as the other ingredients.

3 Peel the fried peppers, put the pulp into a mortar (or blender) together with the almonds and hazelnuts, bread crumbs and the peeled cloves of garlic, and blend to a paste. Transfer the paste to a bowl, season with a pinch of hot pimiento, salt and pepper, and a few drops of vinegar.

4 Blend in very slowly – drop by drop, and stirring all the time – sufficient oil to obtain a smooth, creamy sauce. Place in the fridge for about one hour and serve as a dip for the prawns.

Romesco sauce is also excellent for serving with white and red meats, fish and vegetables. If more oil is added to make the sauce thinner, it becomes an ideal salad dressing, or it can be added even to shellfish and seafood during cooking to make the dish richer. If dried sweet peppers are not available (it is difficult to find them outside of Spain) a large and fresh sweet red pepper can be used after grilling it to remove the skin. The sauce can be made even hotter by adding dried pimientos (fried in the pan together with the dried or fresh pepper), or milder by adding the pulp of a ripe cooking tomato.

| Prawn tails, 500 g (1 lb 2 oz)
Parsley (for garnish)
Salt and pepper

For the salsa romesco
2 dried sweet peppers | (See opposite page)
Almond and hazelnut kernels, 6U g (2 oz; 1/3 cup)
Hot pimiento powder (*pimentón fuerte*)
3-4 cloves of garlic | 1 slice of stale bread without crust
Vinegar
Olive oil

Serves: 6-8
Preparation: 20'+1h | **Cooking: 20'**
Difficulty: ●
Flavour: ● ● ●
Kcal (per serving): 256
Proteins (per serving): 15
Fats (per serving): 16
Nutritional value: ● ● ● |

PATATAS BRAVAS

Potatoes in spicy sauce

5-6 medium-sized potatoes
1 onion
2 cloves of garlic
3 ripe cooking tomatoes
1 dried red pimiento
Half a lemon
Dry white wine
Salt
Olive oil

Serves:	6
Preparation:	20'
Cooking:	30'
Difficulty:	● ●
Flavour:	● ● ●
Kcal (per serving):	297
Proteins (per serving):	5
Fats (per serving):	11
Nutritional value:	● ● ●

1 Rinse, trim and prepare all the vegetables according to their use. Peel, wash and dry the potatoes; dice them then fry them in a pan with 4-5 tablespoons of oil until golden crisp, turning them over frequently. This should take about 15 minutes. Remove the potatoes with a draining spoon and drain on kitchen paper.

2 Finely chop the onion and sauté slowly in a large pan with 2-3 tablespoons of oil; add the peeled and chopped garlic, the crumbled pimiento (without seeds) and the tomatoes cut into pieces. Pour half a glass of wine over the ingredients in the pan and simmer slowly for about ten minutes, stirring every now and then.

3 Add the fried potatoes, the juice of the half lemon and a pinch of salt; increase the heat under the pan and, stirring to blend all the flavours, allow the sauce to thicken and coat the potatoes. Serve hot, with other *tapas*, remembering to put toothpicks near them for easy handling.

Barcelona, Plaça de Catalunya.

XATO

Tarragona-style salad

1 large head of lettuce
2 ribs of celery
2 ripe cooking tomatoes
4-5 cloves of garlic
1 dried sweet pepper
(see page 14)
Almond and hazelnut
kernels, 60 g
(2 oz; 1/3 cup)
Parsley
Small green and black olives
(for garnish)
Vinegar
Salt
Olive oil

Serves:	6
Preparation:	20'+1h30'
Cooking:	10'
Difficulty:	●
Flavour:	● ● ●
Kcal (per serving):	226
Proteins (per serving):	4
Fats (per serving):	21
Nutritional value:	● ●

1 Soak the dried pepper for half an hour before starting to prepare the salad (if dried sweet peppers are unavailable, use a tablespoon of mild ground pimiento, or *pimentón dulce*, mixed with a little water). Blanch the almonds and hazelnuts in unsalted boiling water for 3-4 minutes; drain then remove the skins.

2 Rinse, trim, and prepare the vegetables according to their use. When preparing the lettuce, rinse and dry it well, remove the stump of the stalk then the tough outer leaves, but do not discard them: these must be cut in half lengthwise and trimmed top and bottom so they can be used as 'bowls' for the *xato* – at least a dozen will be needed.

3 Roast the tomatoes and the cloves of garlic under the grill of the oven; remove from the oven and peel both tomatoes and garlic. Put these in a mortar (or blender) with the drained and seeded sweet pepper, the almonds and hazelnuts and a sprig of parsley, then blend to a paste; put this paste in a bowl and add a pinch of salt, 4-5 tablespoons of oil and a few drops of vinegar.

4 If the resulting sauce appears too thick, dilute it with a little water. Tear the lettuce to shreds and put it in a salad bowl with the celery stalks cut into strips; pour the sauce over the salad, toss and leave to stand for one hour. Thereafter, toss the salad once more and distribute amongst the little lettuce bowls. Garnish with olives and serve with other *tapas* or as hors d'œuvres.

CIGALAS AL AJO

Garlic scampi

Scampi, 1 Kg (2 ¹/₄ lb)
4-5 small, fresh pimientos
One head of garlic
Salt and pepper
Olive oil

Serves: 8	
Preparation: 15′	
Cooking: 3′	
Difficulty: ●	
Flavour: ●●●	
Kcal (per serving): 237	
Proteins (per serving): 20	
Fats (per serving): 16	
Nutritional value: ●●●	

1 Prepare the scampi taking care to eliminate the shell and dorsal vein (intestine), rinse and dry. Rinse and prepare the pimientos by removing the stalks and seeds, dry and chop into tiny pieces (if dried pimientos are used, just remove the seeds). Peel the garlic cloves and slice each lengthwise into four.

2 Toss the scampi, pimientos and garlic in a frying pan with 5-6 tablespoons of oil for 3 minutes, adding salt and pepper to taste. Serve immediately.

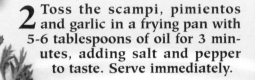

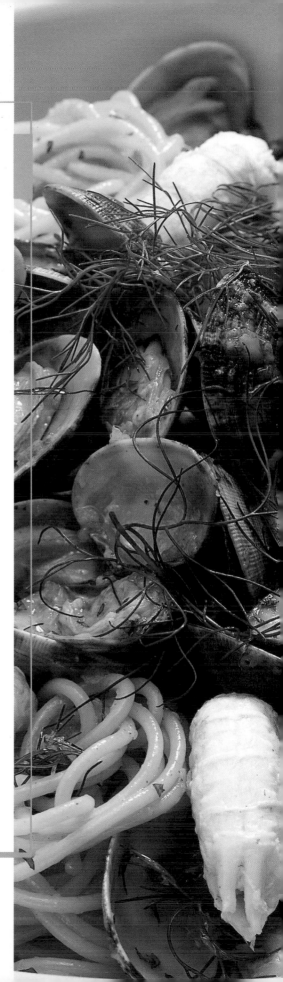

Rice, Pasta and Soups

Rich and delicate cannelloni,
pasta and rice with fish and seafood,
or with meat, vegetables and cured meats:
each recipe more irresistible than the one before.
However, the reader will soon realise
that these are not all merely first courses:
in fact, most of them can be considered
all-in-one meals that can be completed
with a salad or some other accompaniment.

2

ARROS AMB CROSTA

Oven-browned rice

Rice for timbales,
  500 g (¹/₂ lb; 2 ³/₄ cups)
6 eggs
Butifarra (see right margin),
  120 g (4 ¹/₂ oz)
Leftover cooked white
  or red meat, 150 g (6 oz)
Lean pork, 100 g (4 oz)
2 ripe tomatoes
Cooked chickpeas,
  100 g (4 oz)
Chicken or vegetable broth
  (made with bouillon cubes),
  1.5 litres (2 ¹/₂ pt)
1 sachet of saffron powder
Salt and pepper
Olive oil

Serves: 6	
Preparation: 15′	
Cooking: 40′	
Difficulty:	● ●
Flavour:	● ●
Kcal (per serving): 739	
Proteins (per serving): 31	
Fats (per serving): 33	
Nutritional value:	● ● ●

1 Slice the *butifarra* into rounds and gently fry them in an earthenware casserole (ovenproof) with 5-6 tablespoons of oil, turning them over so that they brown on both sides. Remove with a draining spoon and keep in a warm place. Remove the seeds from the tomatoes, chop the pulp and gently fry for five minutes in the oil left in the casserole, together with the diced lean pork. Add the rice and the hot broth; flavour with salt and pepper to taste, adding a sachet of saffron. Mix well.

2 Bring to the boil then lower the heat to minimum; add the browned *butifarra*, the left over meat and the chickpeas. Simmer, mixing every now and then, until the rice is just cooked (*al dente*) but not soft; this will take approx. 15 minutes. Remove the pan from the heat, smooth the surface of the rice and cover it with the eggs beaten with a pinch of salt. Place in a heated oven (200°C; 375°F) until the egg mixture is cooked and the surface is golden brown.

Butifarra is a cured sausage typical of the Catalonia and Eastern regions, but is found all over Spain. Butifarra blanca is a fat, juicy but firm sausage (like a Scottish white pudding) made of minced pork (loin fillet and belly) and – sometimes – onion, garlic, cinnamon, cloves and wine, and can be pan-cooked or grilled (it can be substituted with other types of spiced sausage, as long as they are not hot in flavour). Butifarra negra, which is not so common, contains pig blood (rather like a 'black pudding') and chopped mint.

ARROS A BANDA

Rice with fish

Rinse and dry the king shrimps. Peel the onion and cloves of garlic; rinse the tomatoes and remove their seeds. Prepare the fish for use: rinse well, remove the scales, then gut and trim them but keep the heads, bones, fins and cartilages to one side. Scrape the mussels and remove their 'beards', then put the mussels in a pan with enough water to just cover them; cover with a lid and allow them to open over gentle heat. Remove from the stove but leave the mussels in their cooking water and keep them warm. Put all the fish trimmings in a pot with about 2.5 litres (4 ¼ pints) of cold water, one of the onions cut into slices, one tomato cut into small pieces, the bouquet garni and a pinch of salt.

Cover with a lid and bring to the boil, lower the heat and simmer for 45'; filter the broth (eliminate the bouquet garni and the vegetables as well as the fish trimmings) and put it back into the pot; bring it back to boiling point. Blanch the shrimps in the boiling broth for about 3-4'; scoop them out, drain and keep in a warm place. At this point, add the fish, cut into pieces, to the broth and gently boil for about 10'; remove the pieces of fish, drain and keep these warm as well. Chop the remaining onion and garlic and sauté in an ovenproof casserole with 4-5 tablespoons of oil; add the other diced tomato and allow the flavours to mix briefly. Add the rice, increase the heat under the casserole and let the rice fry a little (stir well); dilute the saffron in the cooking liquid from the mussels and pour this broth over the rice. Season with salt and cook over medium heat for 15', adding a ladle of warm fish broth every now and then. Put the casserole in the oven pre-heated to 200°C (400°F) for 10'. Serve the rice garnished with the mussels and shrimps; put the fish pieces in a separate serving dish with the *alioli* sauce as accompaniment.

Risotto rice, 400 g
  (14 oz; 2 ³/4 cups)
Mixed white-flesh
  Mediterranean fish
  (sea bass, grey mullet,
  grouper, frog fish, gurnard
  or scorpion-fish,
  sea bream, etc.),
  approx. 1 Kg (2 lbs)
6 large king shrimps
24 mussels
2 onions
2 cloves of garlic
2 ripe tomatoes
Bouquet garni, tied
  (bay leaf, oregano, parsley
  and thyme)
1 sachet of saffron powder
Alioli sauce,
  for accompaniment
  (see page 72)
Salt and pepper, olive oil

Serves:	6
Preparation:	30'
Cooking:	1h30'
Difficulty:	● ● ●
Flavour:	● ● ●
Kcal (per serving):	477
Proteins (per serving):	32
Fats (per serving):	12
Nutritional value:	● ●

Costa Brava.

23

ARROS NEGRE AMB ALL I OLI

Black rice with garlic and oil sauce

1 Scrape the shells of the mussels, remove their 'beards', rinse and put into a pan; add sufficient water to just cover the mussels, put the lid on the pan and allow the valves to open over intense heat. As soon as all the mussels have opened (eliminate any that

have failed to open), remove from the stove; extract the flesh from the mussels, keep to one side but discard the shells; do not throw away the cooking water.

2 Prepare the squids (or cuttlefish): gut them (keep 4-5 of the ink sacs), rinse well and, separating the tentacles from the bodies (leave them whole if they are very small), cut them into pieces. Rinse and trim the vegetables according to their use; sauté the chopped onion and the finely diced sweet pepper in a casserole (preferably earthenware) with 5-6 tablespoons of oil. Add the squids and cook over medium heat for 3-4'.

3 Add the rinsed cherry tomatoes and cook for 4-5'. Filter the mussel cooking water into the casserole, lower the heat and simmer for about 20' to reduce the liquid. Add the rice and about one litre/1 pint of hot water; season with salt and add the fresh pimiento kept whole. Stir occasionally as the rice simmers and add more hot water whenever necessary.

*Barcelona, Casa Milà, **better known as 'La Pedrera', designed by Antonio Gaudí.***

Risotto rice, 250 g (8 oz; 2 ½ cups)	Cherry tomatoes, 150 g (5-6 oz)	Serves: 4	Proteins (per serving): 31
Squids or tiny cuttlefish, approx. 500 g (1 lb)	3 cloves of garlic	Preparation: 25'	Fats (per serving): 14
Mussels, 500 g (1 lb 2 oz)	1 fresh red pimiento	Cooking: 1h	Nutritional value: ● ●
Shrimp tails, 100 g (4 oz)	Dry white wine	Difficulty: ● ● ●	
1 onion	Salt	Flavour: ● ●	
1 green sweet pepper	Olive oil	Kcal (per serving): 534	

4 In the meantime, prepare the sauce: pound the peeled garlic cloves with a pinch of salt in a mortar, put the resulting paste into a bowl and stir in a glass of oil. Dilute the ink from the sacs in half a glass of wine and add to the casserole when the rice has cooked for 15'. Stir well. After about 5' (make sure the rice is cooked *al dente*) remove the casserole from the heat; add the shelled mussels, the shrimp tails and a tablespoon of the garlic sauce. Stir gently and serve, putting the remaining sauce in a bowl for accompaniment.

FIDEOS A LA CATALANA

Spicy spaghetti with cured meats ▶

Cut the spare-ribs into tiny pieces and brown them in the melted lard in a casserole (preferably earthenware); when nicely browned, add the chopped onion and allow to stew slowly. Add the chopped tomatoes (without seeds) and a pinch of ground pimiento; allow the flavours to blend for about 4-5 minutes. Skin the sausage and crumble the meat into the casserole along with the *butifarra* cut into disks and the broth; bring to the boil and add the pasta. Lower the heat to minimum. Ground in a mortar (or in a food mixer) the hazelnuts, almonds, pine nuts and garlic, adding the saffron, a pinch of cinnamon, a sprig of parsley and 2 tablespoons of breadcrumbs; dilute the paste obtained with a little broth and add this mixture to the soup simmering in the casserole. Remove from the heat when the pasta is almost cooked (*al dente*) and serve; flakes of mature cheese may be sprinkled over the soup before serving.

Rice, 400 g
(14 oz; 2 3/4 cups)
1 chicken breast
Half a saddle of rabbit
Pork spare-ribs,
600 g (1 1/4 lb)
3 pork sausages
Butifarra blanca
(see page 22), 250 g (9 oz)
24 large clams
2 squids
1 onion
2 ripe tomatoes
Mild pimiento powder
(*pimentón dulce*)
2 cloves of garlic
Rind of half a lemon
Parsley
Vegetable broth (ready
made), half a litre (1 pint)
Salt and pepper
Olive oil

Serves: 6	
Preparation: 20'	
Cooking: 40'	
Difficulty:	●●
Flavour:	●●
Kcal (per serving): 617	
Proteins (per serving): 34	
Fats (per serving): 28	
Nutritional value:	●●●

ARROS A LA CATALÀ

Catalan-style rice

Peel the onion and rinse the tomatoes, splitting them open to remove the seeds. Prepare the squids by removing the internal cuttlebone, the ink sacs, eyes and 'beaks'; slice the bodies into rings and chop the tentacles. Soak the clams in slightly salted water to eliminate all impurities; rinse under cold running water then allow them to open in a pan, with a little water, over low heat (discard any that have failed to open). Bone the chicken breast and eliminate the cartilages, then cut the meat into strips. Chop the rabbit into bite-size pieces (be careful not to splinter the bones). Divide the spare-ribs into small segments. Brown the chicken breast, rabbit and spare-ribs in a casserole with 5-6 tablespoons of oil; add the chopped onion, then the squids together with a pinch of salt and pepper. Stirring, sauté gently for 7-8'; add the diced tomatoes then the *butifarra* and sausages broken up into small pieces. Let the flavours mix for a further 6-7' then add the rice and a teaspoon of *pimentón*; fry for a few minutes over intense heat. Lower the heat to medium and gradually add ladles of the hot broth. Stir frequently and taste for salt. After 10' cooking time, sprinkle the rice with the chopped garlic and parsley and add the clams. After a further 10', remove the casserole from the stove, sprinkle grated lemon rind over the rice and serve.

Fideos (thin or ribbon spaghetti), 350 g (14 oz) Pork spare-ribs, 200 g (8 oz) *Butifarra* (see page 22), 100 g (4 oz)	1 pimiento sausage 1 onion, 1 clove of garlic 2 ripe tomatoes Ground pimiento and cinnamon Parsley 1 sachet of saffron powder	Shelled and blanched hazelnuts, almonds and pine-nuts (1 tbsp of each) Chicken broth (ready made), 1.5 litres (2 1/2 pt)	Dry breadcrumbs Mature cheese for grating (optional) Lard, 30 g (1 oz; 3 tbsp) Serves: 4 Preparation: 20'	**Cooking: 30'** **Difficulty: ● ●** **Flavour: ● ●** **Kcal (per serving): 762** **Proteins (per serving): 33** **Fats (per serving): 36** **Nutritional value: ● ● ●**

FIDEUA

Paella with pasta and fish ▶

Fideos (spaghetti, or other
 types of long pasta),
 400 g (14 oz)
Frogfish (one piece,
 skinned), 400 g (14 oz)
6 scampi (or king shrimps)
1 onion
4 ripe tomatoes
2 cloves of garlic
Hot pimiento powder
 (*pimentón fuerte*)
Fish broth (made with
 appropriate bullion cubes),
 about half a litre (1 pint)
Parsley
Curly parsley (for garnish)
1 sachet of saffron powder
Salt and pepper
Olive oil

Serves:	4-6
Preparation:	15'
Cooking:	30'
Difficulty:	●●
Flavour:	●●●
Kcal (per serving):	549
Proteins (per serving):	30
Fats (per serving):	18
Nutritional value:	●●

Peel the onion, rinse the tomatoes and cut them open to remove the seeds. Rinse and dry the scampi then toss-fry them for about 3-4 minutes in 5-6 tablespoons of very hot oil in the *paellera* pan (see page 46); remove them with a draining spoon, drain and keep in a warm place. Lower the heat under the pan and slowly cook the sliced onion and the frogfish cut into bite-size pieces in the oil used for the scampi; stir gently. As soon as the fish begins to colour, add a sprig of parsley finely chopped together with the peeled garlic, the diced tomatoes, salt, pepper and a teaspoon of *pimentón*; stir very gently and allow the flavours to mix. After about 5-6 minutes cooking time, add the *fideos* to the *paellera*, making sure the strands do not overlap; dilute the saffron in the boiling hot broth and pour a sufficient amount over the ingredients to cover them. Bring back to the boil then lower the heat to medium; cook for 10-12 minutes, adding more hot broth whenever necessary. One minute before the end of the cooking time, arrange the scampi over the *fideua* (which should be fairly dry). When ready, allow the ingredients to cool slightly then serve in the *paellera*, garnishing with sprigs of curly parsley.

ARROZ CON HABAS

Rice with broad beans

Soup rice, 240 g
 (8 oz; 2 1/2 cups)
Fresh broad beans, shelled,
 300 g (12 oz; 1 2/3 cup)
Raw cured ham (*jamón
 serrano*), 100 g (4 oz)
 in one piece
Lard (or bacon), 80 g (3 oz)
 in one piece
Vegetable broth, 1 litre
 (2 pints); salt; olive oil

Serves:	4
Preparation:	10'
Cooking:	40'
Difficulty:	●
Flavour:	●●
Kcal (per serving):	697
Proteins (per serving):	16
Fats (per serving):	46
Nutritional value:	●●●

Dice the ham and lard and slowly sauté in a casserole with 3-4 tablespoons of oil; add the rinsed and dried broad beans, half a litre/1 pint of hot broth, then season with salt and cover. Simmer for about 15 minutes then add the rice. Stir well and allow the rice to absorb the liquid, cooking for about 20 minutes and adding more hot broth whenever necessary (the mixture should remain rather liquid). Remove from the stove and allow to rest a few minutes before serving.

FIDEOS CON MARISCOS

Thin spaghetti with seafood

Fideos (thin or fine ribbon-
   spaghetti), 350 g (12 oz)
Scampi (or king prawns),
   600 g (1 ¼ lb)
Large clams, 500 g
   (1 lb 2 oz)
1 onion
1 ripe cooking tomato
2 cloves of garlic
Sprigs of wild fennel
   (plus some for garnish)
Bay leaf
Parsley
Ground mild pimiento
   (*pimentón dulce*)
1 sachet of saffron powder
Dry white wine
Salt and pepper
Olive oil

Serves: 4-6	
Preparation: 25'	
Cooking: 1h	
Difficulty:	● ●
Flavour:	● ● ●
Kcal (per serving): 485	
Proteins (per serving): 21	
Fats (per serving): 12	
Nutritional value:	● ● ●

1 Rinse and prepare all vegetables and herbs according to their use. Rinse the scampi (or prawns) and blanch them for 5-6 minutes in approximately 2.5 litres (4 ½ pints) of slightly salted boiling water; drain (keeping the cooking water), remove the shells (of all but two, which will be used as garnish) and intestinal tract but keep the heads, claws (if scampi are used) and shells, which must be put back into the pot containing the water where the seafood was cooked. Add a quarter of the onion to this water, as well as a sprig of parsley, a few sprigs of wild fennel, a bay leaf and half a glass of wine. Bring to the boil and simmer for about half an hour; filter through a fine sieve into a pot and discard all solids, including the remains of the seafood.

2 Dilute the seafood broth, if necessary, with a little water, bring to the boil, taste for salt and toss in the *fideos*; boil for four-fifths of the cooking time indicated on the packet then drain.

3 In the meantime, sauté the remaining onion, chopped fine, in an earthenware casserole with 3-4 tablespoons of oil; add the peeled and crushed cloves of garlic, the tomato cut up roughly, a few sprigs of wild fennel, salt, pepper and a teaspoon of *pimentón*, then the saffron diluted in a little wine.

4 Add the drained clams (see page 26, *Arros a la català*) and allow the valves to open in the sauce, discarding any clams that have failed to open. Pour the drained pasta into the casserole, add a few tablespoons of the cooking broth and the scampi or prawn tails; toss over high heat to blend all flavours rapidly. Serve the *fideos* sprinkled with chopped parsley and a few sprigs of wild fennel.

CANELONES A LA CATALANA

Catalan-style cannelloni

Cannelloni (see right margin),
   350 g (³/4 lb)
Lean pork, 200 g (¹/2 lb)
Boned chicken breast,
   250 g (10 oz)
4-5 chicken livers
Lean raw cured ham
   (in one piece), 70 g (3 oz)
1 onion
2-3 ripe cooking tomatoes
Mature *mahón* or *manchego*
   cheese (or substitute with
   Parmesan), 80 g (3 ¹/2 oz)
Dry white wine
Salt and pepper
Cooking fat, 30 g
   (1 ¹/4 oz; 2 tbsp)
Butter, 50 g (1 ³/4 oz; 3 tbsp)

For the béchamel *sauce*
Plain flour, 40 g
   (1 ¹/2 oz; 3 tbsp)
Full milk, ¹/2 litre (1 pint)
Grated nutmeg
Salt and pepper
Butter, 50 g (1 ³/4 oz; 3 tbsp)

Serves: 4	
Preparation: 25'	
Cooking: 1h10'	
Difficulty: ●●●	
Flavour: ●●	
Kcal (per serving): 1202	
Proteins (per serving): 50	
Fats (per serving): 65	
Nutritional value: ●●●	

1 Rinse the tomatoes, cut them in two horizontally, remove the seeds then put to one side. Peel and chop the onion and sauté it slowly in a pan with the melted cooking fat; add the roughly chopped meats (including the rinsed and dried chicken livers, but not the ham), then half a glass of wine which must evaporate over medium heat. Lower the heat under the pan and brown the ingredients for about ten minutes, seasoning with salt and pepper. Remove the meats with a draining spoon, finely grind them in a food processor then put the mince in a bowl.

2 To prepare the *béchamel* sauce, melt the butter in a small pot then gradually add the flour, stirring all the time. When the *roux* becomes the colour of pale straw, season with salt, pepper and a pinch of grated nutmeg then gradually add the milk while continuing to stir. Simmer gently, still stirring, for about twenty minutes.

3 Spread a fairly thick layer of *béchamel* over the bottom of an oven dish greased with 20 g (³/4 oz/1 tbsp) of butter. Fold 2-3 tablespoons of *béchamel* into the minced meats and stuff the cannelloni with this mixture. Arrange them side by side over the *béchamel* already in the oven dish and cover them with the remaining sauce.

4 Garnish with rounds of sliced tomato and sprinkle with the diced ham. Put the remaining butter in flakes over the top, dust with grated cheese and bake in the oven, preheated to 180°C (350°F); the cannelloni will be ready when the surface has a golden crust (this will take at least half an hour).

Ready-to-use cannelloni (requiring no cooking before stuffing and baking) can be found quite easily. However, if these are not available, the rectangles of pasta used for making lasagne may be used instead: soften them a little in boiling water, drain then spread them out on a clean kitchen cloth to dry; place the stuffing in the middle of each rectangle and roll them into shape, arranging them in the oven dish with the loose end of the pasta underneath and covering them with the sauce and other ingredients as indicated before baking. In the past, the traditional stuffing was often enriched with lamb's brain blanched in boiling water then browned with the other types of meat, but since this ingredient is not often enjoyed it can be eliminated from the recipe quite easily.

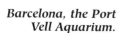
***Barcelona, the Port
Vell Aquarium.***

SOPA DE MEJILLONES

Mussel soup

Mussels, 1 Kg (2 lbs 2 oz)
1 onion
3-4 ripe tomatoes
3 cloves of garlic
Parsley
Ground cinnamon
Aniseed liqueur or brandy
Slices of toasted farmhouse
    bread
    (served with the soup)
Salt and pepper
Olive oil

Serves: 4	
Preparation: 20'	
Cooking: 30'	
Difficulty: ●●	
Flavour: ●●●	
Kcal (per serving): 438	
Proteins (per serving): 16	
Fats (per serving): 12	
Nutritional value: ●●	

1 Scrape the mussel shells and pull out the 'beards'; rinse the mussels and put them in a pan with sufficient water to just cover them. Put the lid on and allow the valves to open over intense heat. As soon as they open remove them from the pan (eliminate any that have failed to open), extract the flesh and discard the shells. Keep the cooking liquid.

2 Peel and slice the onion then slowly sauté it in 5-6 tablespoons of oil in an earthenware casserole; add the rinsed tomatoes (without seeds and cut into pieces) and allow to stew for about 15 minutes. Squash the tomatoes to a paste with the back of a wooden spoon.

3 Add the peeled and crushed cloves of garlic, a sprig of parsley (chopped) and a pinch of ground cinnamon. Pour a small glass of liqueur over the ingredients. Season with salt and pepper to taste.

4 Filter the mussel cooking liquid into the casserole, bring to the boil, stir and allow the sauce to thicken a little; lower the heat and add the mussels. Cook for 4-5 minutes then remove from the stove. Sprinkle chopped parsley over the soup and serve with slices of toasted bread.

POTAJE A LA CATALANA

Chickpea soup

Dried chickpeas, 350 g
  (12 oz; 1 3/4 cup)
Butifarra blanca
  (see page 22), 100 g (4 oz)
2 eggs
2-3 ripe cooking tomatoes
1 onion
Bay leaf
Pine nuts, 30 g (1 oz; 2 tbsp)
Salt and pepper
Cooking fat, 30 g
  (1 oz; 2 tbsp)

Serves: 4
Preparation: 15'+6h
Cooking: 1h30'
Difficulty: ● ●
Flavour: ● ●
Kcal (per serving): 545
Proteins (per serving): 29
Fats (per serving): 22
Nutritional value: ● ● ●

S oak the chickpeas for 5-6 hours before starting to prepare the
soup; drain them, put them in a pot and cover them with cold
water (approx. 2 litres, 3½ pints), add a quarter of the onion and the
bay leaf. Put the lid on the pot, bring to the boil and simmer over
lowest heat for 1¼ hours. In the meantime, rinse and roughly chop
the tomatoes. Hard boil the eggs in a small pan for 7 minutes; leave
to cool for a few minutes then shell them.
Finely chop the remaining onion and sauté in the cooking fat in an
earthenware casserole; add the chopped tomatoes, the pine nuts
and the diced *butifarra*. Simmer very slowly for about fifteen minutes, stirring frequently and seasoning with salt and pepper; add the
chickpeas and enough of the cooking broth to obtain a rather thick
soup. Slowly simmer the *potaje* for a further quarter of an hour and
serve hot, garnished with slices of boiled egg.

Meat
AND FOWL

Elegant recipes that skilfully combine
lobster and chicken, mussels
and pork, snails and rabbit:
all worthy companions to the traditional
escudella i carn d'olla
which offers a full meal consisting in soup,
second course and accompaniment,
and the exquisite pavo a la catalana.
Then, of course, there is the ever-present paella
of which Catalonia has its own, delicious version.

3

ASADO DE CERDO A LA CATALANA

Oven-roasted fillet of pork ▶

1 Pound the peeled garlic to obtain a paste and rub this all over the pork bound with string. Leave the meat to stand on a plate for about one hour then brown it on low heat in an ovenproof earthenware casserole with the melted lard, turning it over now and then to brown evenly on all sides. After rinsing the vegetables, chop the onion and cut the celery into tiny pieces, and add them to the casserole with 2 bay leaves, a sprig each of thyme, oregano and parsley, a small piece of cinnamon, the cloves, and a generous dusting of freshly ground pepper.

2 Put the casserole in the oven heated to 220°C (410°F) for 5 minutes then lower the heat to 180°C (350°F); pour a glass of the wine over the meat and continue cooking for about 1½ hours. Every now and then, check to see that the meat does not dry out and, in this case, baste it with its juice or if necessary, add a few tablespoons of hot water. Taste for salt. When the meat is done, remove from the oven and allow it to stand for a few minutes; remove the string and serve it sliced, with its own gravy (skimmed of fat) in a sauceboat. Serve with potatoes, spinach or turnip tops.

Pork spare-ribs, approx.
  1.2 Kg (2 ½ lbs)
2-3 chicken livers
Minced lean pork,
  100 g (4 oz)
2 fresh pork sausages
1 small onion, half a celery
  rib, 1 cooking apple
Dried apricots and prunes,
  100 g (4 oz)
Sultanas, 20 g (¾ oz; 1 tbsp)
Pine-nuts, 20 g (¾ oz;1 tbsp)
5 large chestnuts
Ground cinnamon
Dry breadcrumbs,
  20 g (¾ oz; 1 tbsp)
Dry white wine
Salt and pepper
Cooking fat, 30 g
  (1 ¼ oz; 2 tbsp)

Serves:	4
Preparation:	15'+30'
Cooking:	1h45'
Difficulty:	●●
Flavour:	●●●
Kcal (per serving):	695
Proteins (per serving):	46
Fats (per serving):	35
Nutritional value:	●●●

COSTILLAS AL HORNO

Oven-roasted pork spare-ribs

Half an hour before starting to prepare the meal, soak the apricots and prunes (pitted) with the sultanas in lukewarm water.
Make a slit in the chestnut skins with a sharp knife and roast them in the oven, then peel off the skins when ready. Clean and trim the vegetables; peel the apple and remove the core.
Gently sauté the trimmed chicken livers for 5 minutes in a pan containing the melted fat; drain and finely chop. Use the fat left in the pan to sauté the onion chopped together with the celery; add the crumbled sausages and the minced pork and slowly brown. Add the chopped chicken livers, the apple cut into pieces, the chopped chestnuts, the drained and chopped apricots and prunes, the sultanas squeezed of all liquid, the pine-nuts, a pinch of cinnamon, salt and pepper, and lastly, the breadcrumbs. Mix all together, pour half a glass of wine over the ingredients, then allow the liquid to reduce slowly for about 10 minutes. Spread the mixture evenly over the bottom of an ovenproof dish (with lid), arrange the slightly salted spare-ribs (cut to suitable serving lengths) on top, pressing them down a little so that they sink into the mixture. Put the lid on the casserole and bake in the oven preheated to 180°C/350°F for about one and a half hours. Remove the lid during the last few minutes of cooking, then serve.

		Serves: 6	Fats (per serving): 15
Boned saddle of pork, 1 Kg (2 ¼ lb)	Bay leaf, oregano, parsley, thyme	Preparation: 15′ +1h	Nutritional value: ● ● ●
1 onion	Dry Jerez wine (Xeres or Sherry)	Cooking: 1h40′	
1 stalk of celery		Difficulty: ● ●	
3 cloves of garlic	Salt and freshly ground pepper	Flavour: ● ●	
Cinnamon		Kcal (per serving): 375	
2 cloves	Lard, 25 g (1 oz; 2 tbsp)	Proteins (per serving): 33	

Ingredients

1 rabbit (with its liver)
   ready for cooking,
   about 1.3 Kg (2 ³/₄ lb)
New potatoes,
   500 g (1 lb 2 oz)
1 onion
2-3 ripe tomatoes
2 cloves of garlic
Bouquet garni, tied
   (bay leaf, parsley, thyme
   and rosemary)
Sprig of parsley
Nutmeg
Fennel seeds
Saffron
1 dry red pimiento
1 piece of dark chocolate
   (or unsweetened cocoa
   powder), 20 g (1 oz)
Plain flour
Red wine
Salt and pepper
Olive oil

Serves:	4
Preparation:	25'
Cooking:	1h
Difficulty:	●●
Flavour:	●●●
Kcal (per serving):	587
Proteins (per serving):	61
Fats (per serving):	21
Nutritional value:	●●

CONEJO AL ESTILO TARRACONENSE

Rabbit and chocolate casserole

1 Rinse and dry the rabbit and cut it into about twenty small pieces (eliminate the head): brown these pieces and the liver evenly in an earthenware casserole with 6 tablespoons of oil. As soon as the rabbit is browned, remove the liver (keep it to one side) and add the chopped onion. When the onion has become soft, add the chopped tomatoes (without seeds); stew a few minutes to let the flavours blend, stirring all the time, then add one and a half glasses of wine, the bouquet garni, a teaspoon of fennel seeds, salt and pepper, and a little grated nutmeg. Cover the casserole, lower the heat to minimum and simmer for about 30 minutes.

2 In the meantime, peel the potatoes (or if they are new, rub them well under running water but do not remove the skins) and cook them in slightly salted boiling water for about 5 minutes; drain them and cut them in half (or if they are very small, leave them whole). Toast a tablespoon of flour by sprinkling it over the bottom of a dry, ungreased pan on low heat, gently shaking the pan until the flour becomes a nutty colour. Pound the liver in a mortar (or in a food mixer) with a pinch of saffron, the dry pimiento without its seeds, the garlic, the chocolate and the toasted flour. Dilute this paste with half a glass of warm water and add it to the rabbit in the casserole. Add the potatoes and mix gently. Put the lid back on the casserole and simmer for a further 20 minutes, until the rabbit meat is tender. Remove the bouquet garni and serve the rabbit sprinkled with chopped parsley.

CONEJO CON CARACOLES

Rabbit with snails

Boil the snails following the instructions given in the recipe on page 60 (*Caracoles a la patarrallada*). Clean and trim the vegetables and herbs according to their use. Prepare the *sofrito*: finely chop the onion, garlic and parsley together then gently sauté them in a pan with 3-4 tablespoons of oil. Add the roughly chopped tomatoes and allow the flavours to mix very slowly, stirring, until the tomatoes are tender. Remove from the heat and keep in a warm place. Cut the rabbit into approximately 20 pieces; quickly brown the pieces in a casserole (with lid) with 5 tablespoons of oil and a pinch of salt. When they are golden brown, add the broth, cover the casserole, lower the heat and simmer for 30 minutes. In the meantime, prepare the *picada*: toast the almonds in the oven, remove the skins then pound the kernels to a paste in a mortar (or food processor) with the garlic, pine nuts and a sprig of parsley; add the cocoa powder, a drop of wine and mix thoroughly. Add both the *sofrito* and the *picada* to the rabbit in the casserole and stir. Lastly, add the snails, taste for salt, and simmer for another half hour with the lid on. Allow the ingredients to cool for a few minutes before serving.

1 rabbit (ready for use), approx. 1.2 Kg (2 1/2 lbs)
Boiled land snails (see page 60), 400 g (14 oz)
Chicken or beef broth (ready-made), approx. half a litre (1 pint)
Salt, olive oil

For the picada
Shelled almonds, 80 g (3 oz)
Dark unsweetened cocoa powder, 40 g (1 1/2 oz; 3 tbsp)
Pine nuts, 30 g (1 1/4 oz; 2 tbsp)
2 cloves of garlic
Parsley
Dry white wine

For the sofrito
1 onion
2 ripe tomatoes
2 cloves of garlic
Parsley
Olive oil

Serves:	4
Preparation:	20'
Cooking:	1h15'
Difficulty:	● ●
Flavour:	● ● ●
Kcal (per serving):	856
Proteins (per serving):	70
Fats (per serving):	50
Nutritional value:	● ● ●

Barcelona's 'unfinished Cathedral' designed by A. Gaudi and dedicated to the Sacred Family.

ESTOFAT DE BOU

Beef stew with chocolate

1 Rinse and prepare the vegetables according to their use. Dice the piece of lard and sauté it slowly in a pan with the melted cooking fat; when the lard starts to melt add the finely chopped carrot and onion, the peeled and crushed cloves of garlic, stirring gently for 2-3 minutes to allow the flavours to mix. Sprinkle the flour over the ingredients and blend it gently into the sauce; remove from the stove and keep in a warm place.

2 Cut the beef into even-sized strips, put them in a casserole (preferably earthenware with a lid) and brown them over intense heat with 3-4 tablespoons of oil; when the strips are evenly browned, season with salt and pepper and pour half a glass of wine over them, allowing it to evaporate.

3 Add the mixture of lard and vegetables, the bouquet garni (tied) and cover with broth containing a further half glass of wine; put the lid on the casserole, bring to the boil, lower the heat to minimum and simmer for three-quarters of an hour.

4 Add the roughly chopped tomato and the spring onions cut into small pieces; cover the casserole again and simmer once more for just under half an hour. At this point, remove the lid and quickly reduce the gravy; add the grated chocolate (or the equivalent weight of bitter cocoa powder) and stir gently to blend the flavours. Remove the bouquet garni and serve the *estofat* garnished with sprigs of parsley and accompanied by oven-roasted new potatoes.

42

Lean beef,
  700 g (1 1/2 lb)
Lard (in one piece),
  100 g (4 oz)
1 onion
Half a carrot
1 ripe cooking tomato
5 cloves of garlic
2 spring onions

Bouquet garni
  (bay leaf, thyme,
  parsley, small piece
  of cinnamon, a couple
  of strips of lemon rind)
Parsley
  (for garnish)
Plain flour,
  10 g (1/2 oz; 3/4 tbsp)

Dark chocolate (one
  piece), 30 g (1 1/4 oz)
Ready-made chicken
  (or vegetable) broth,
  approx. 1.5 litres
  (2 1/2 pints)
Oven-roasted
  new potatoes
  (for accompaniment)

Red wine
Salt and pepper
Cooking fat,
  25 g (1 oz; 1 3/4 tbsp)
Olive oil

Serves:	4
Preparation:	25'
Cooking:	1h30'
Difficulty:	● ●
Flavour:	● ●
Kcal (per serving):	740
Proteins (per serving):	41
Fats (per serving):	52
Nutritional value:	● ● ●

ESCUDELLA I CARN D'OLLA

Mixed boiled meats with rice and broth soup ▶

About 4-5 hours before starting to prepare the meal, soak the chickpeas in slightly salted water. Prepare the *pilota*: finely chop the lard and put it in a bowl together with the minced pork, the egg, the breadcrumbs, a sprig of parsley finely chopped with the peeled garlic, a pinch each of salt and pepper, and mix thoroughly. Work the mixture into a ball, toss it in flour then put in a cool place. Prepare the meats (beef, hen, ear, snout and trotter) in the usual manner for boiling and put them, together with the lard and the ham bone (sawn into 2-3 pieces), in a large pot with just under 5 litres/9 pints of cold water. Bring to the boil, remove the scum from the surface of the broth, and then add the drained chickpeas. Put the lid on the pot and simmer for one and a half hours. In the meantime, clean and trim the vegetables (carrot, cabbage, turnip and potatoes) according to use. At the end of the 1 ½ hours, add the *butifarra* (cut into small pieces), the vegetables cut into small chunks, and the *pilota*. Put the lid back on the pot and simmer again until the vegetables are cooked (but *al dente*) and the meats are tender.

Filter the broth into a smaller pot and cook the rice in this after adding the sachet of saffron. Serve the rice in the broth as a first course. For the second course, slice or cut the meats (discard the ham bones) and serve them with the vegetables on a platter.

Lean beef (muscle),
   700 g (1 ½ lbs)
Lard, 100 g (4 oz)
Pigskin, 80 g (3 oz)
1 onion, 2 carrots
Fresh shelled peas,
   150 g (5-6 oz; 1 ¼ cup)
2 cloves of garlic
Bouquet garni, tied
   (bay leaf, marjoram,
   parsley and thyme)
Chicken or beef broth
   (ready-made),
   half a litre (1 pint)
Plain flour, 10 g (⅓ oz;
   ¾ tbsp)
Salt and pepper, olive oil

Serves:	4
Preparation:	20'
Cooking:	1h20'
Difficulty:	●●
Flavour:	●●
Kcal (per serving):	709
Proteins (per serving):	46
Fats (per serving):	49
Nutritional value:	●●●

FRICANDÒ

Stewed meat and vegetables

First of all, boil the pigskin for 10 minutes in slightly salted water then drain and scrape the skin. Cut the meat into bite-size pieces, dip them in flour and brown them slowly in a pan with 2 tablespoons of oil together with the skin cut in to strips and the diced lard; keep in a warm place. Rinse and trim the vegetables and herbs according to their use. Sauté the finely chopped onion and garlic in a casserole (preferably earthenware with a lid) in 4-5 tablespoons of oil. Add the meat, pigskin and lard, and season with salt and pepper; stir, then add the carrots sliced into rounds. Stir again and allow the flavours to mix a few minutes, then add the rinsed and drained peas. Cover the ingredients with the hot broth, add the bouquet garni, put the lid on the casserole and bring to the boil. Lower the heat and simmer for about one hour, taking the lid off during the last 10 minutes. Eliminate the bouquet garni and serve the *fricandò* in a warmed platter.

Lean cut of boiling beef (muscle), 500 g (1 lb)	1 pig trotter	*For the* pilota	Parsley	**Serves: 6-8**
Half a boiling hen	Half a ham bone	Lean minced pork, 100 g (4 oz)		**Preparation: 25'+4-5h**
Bacon (in one piece), 150 g (5-6 oz)	Dried chickpeas, 250 g (9 oz; 2 1/2 cups)	Lard, 100 g (4 oz)	*For the soup*	**Cooking: 2h**
Pig ear and snout, 300 g (10 oz)	2-3 potatoes	1 egg	Soup rice (or *fideos*, or tiny pasta shapes suitable	**Difficulty:** ● ●
Butifarra negra, 200 g (8 oz) in one piece (see page 22)	1 carrot	2 cloves of garlic	for broth), 250-280 g, (9 oz; 1 1/4 cup—10 oz; 1 1/2 cups)	**Flavour:** ● ●
	1 cabbage	Plain flour, 10 g (1/3 oz; 3/4 tbsp)	1 sachet of saffron powder	**Kcal (per serving): 1490**
	1 turnip	Dry breadcrumbs, 20 g (2/3 oz; 1 1/2 tbsp)		**Proteins (per serving): 10**
	Salt and pepper			**Fats (per serving): 21**
				Nutritional value: ● ● ●

PAELLA

1 chicken, ready for use,
 1.2 Kg (2 ³/₄ lb)
Risotto rice,
 700 g (1 ¹/₂ lb; 3 ³/₄ cups)
Lean pork, 250 g (10 oz)
6-8 scampi
Fresh clams,
 500 g (1 lb 2 oz)
Shelled peas (even frozen),
 300 g (12 oz)
4-5 ripe tomatoes
2 sweet peppers
1 onion
4-5 cloves of garlic
Bay leaf
1 sachet of saffron powder
1 lemon
Ground pimiento
Chicken broth, approx.
 1 litre (1 ²/₃ pt)
Salt, fresh ground pepper
Olive oil

Serves: 6	
Preparation: 25'	
Cooking: 1h	
Difficulty: ● ●	
Flavour: ● ● ●	
Kcal (per serving): 1107	
Proteins (per serving): 59	
Fats (per serving): 44	
Nutritional value: ● ●	

1 Before starting, roast the peppers under the grill in the oven for about ten minutes, turning them around every now and then, so that they can be skinned easily; remove the stalks, seeds and fibrous parts, then cut into strips. Clean the tomatoes, remove the seeds and chop. Peel the cloves of garlic and the onion and chop finely all together. At this point, cut the chicken into about a dozen pieces and brown in the typical *paellera* (or in another large pan) with 6-7 tablespoons of oil, and a pinch of salt and pepper; when all pieces are golden-brown, remove from the pan and keep in a warm place.

2 Cut the pork into bite-size pieces and brown it in the pan together with the clams (see page 26, *Arros a a la català*) (to open them) and the rinsed scampi (do not dry them beforehand). When the scampi become pinkish, take them and the other ingredients out, and put them in a warm place; eliminate any clams that have not opened.

3 Put the chopped onion and garlic into the oil left in the pan and stew until soft; add the tomatoes and peas and simmer gently for about 5 minutes. Add a bay leaf, a sachet of saffron, a teaspoon of ground pimiento, salt and freshly ground pepper; stir well to combine all the flavours. Add the rice, allow it to absorb the sauce for a couple of minutes, then pour in the boiling hot broth; bring back to the boil, lower the heat and simmer for 20 minutes, until the rice has absorbed all the liquid; check for salt. At this point, add the strips of roasted peppers, mix, and then put the chicken and pork pieces, the scampi, and the clams in their shells, all on top of the rice. Cover the *paellera* with kitchen foil and put in the oven pre-heated to 180°C (350°F) for fifteen minutes. Serve in the *paellera* with wedges of lemon in a separate dish.

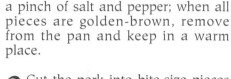

The paella, *known the world over, takes its name from the typical* paellera *(a large, not too deep, two-handled pan) traditionally used for cooking this famous, delicious all-in-one dish. It appears to have been originally a fairly humble dish, one made from various leftovers in the enormous pans of noble kitchens and given to the servants.*

PAELLA *PARELLADA*

Catalan-style *paella*

| Rice, 400 g (12 oz; 2 1/4 cups) |
| Boned chicken (or turkey) breast, 250 g (9 oz) |
| Lean pork, 300 g (10 oz) |
| *Butifarra blanca*, 200 g (8 oz) (see page 22) |
| 1 trimmed slice of frog fish, (angler fish) 300 g (10 oz) |
| 5 medium-sized squids |
| 12 king prawns |
| 1 onion |
| 5 sweet peppers (will also serve as garnish) |
| 5 medium-sized artichokes |
| Shelled fresh peas, 100 g (4 oz) |
| Button mushrooms, 80 g (3 oz) |
| Parsley (for garnish) |
| 1 sachet of saffron powder |
| 1 lemon |
| Salt and pepper |
| Cooking fat, 40 g (1 1/2 oz; 3 tbsp) |

Serves:	6
Preparation:	30'
Cooking:	50'
Difficulty:	● ●
Flavour:	● ● ●
Kcal (per serving):	647
Proteins (per serving):	41
Fats (per serving):	19
Nutritional value:	● ●

1 Prepare the squids by removing the entrails, ink sacs and cartilages; rinse them well under cold running water then dry them. Separate the tentacles from the bodies; chop the former and slice the latter into rings.

2 Rinse, trim and skin the mushrooms, being careful to eliminate all grit. Peel the onion. Prepare the artichokes by removing the tough outer leaves and the stalks (if necessary, clip the tips of the remaining leaves) then blanch them for about 10' in slightly salted boiling water containing the juice of the lemon. Drain the artichokes upside down on kitchen paper. In the meantime, roast the peppers under the grill of the oven until black (requires about 10'), turning them over frequently. Take the peppers from the oven, remove the skins, seeds and fibrous parts, and then cut them into strips.

3 Melt the cooking fat in the *paellera*. Dice the meats and the *butifarra* and brown them slowly together with the squid rings in this fat; when these ingredients start to colour, push them towards the rim of the *paellera*. Cut the frog fish into bite-size pieces and put in the centre of the pan; add the chopped tentacles and simmer slowly for 5-6'.

4 Cut the artichokes into wedges and add to the pan, with the shelled peas, two-thirds of the peppers, and the mushrooms and onion sliced. Stir and allow the flavours to blend for 5' before adding the rice and the rinsed prawns; pour in sufficient warm water to cover, season with salt and pepper, and add the saffron diluted in a little lukewarm water. Cook the rice over medium heat (add a few tablespoons of hot water, if necessary). Serve the *paella* garnished with the remaining peppers and sprigs of parsley.

PAVO A LA CATALANA

Stuffed turkey

1 ready for use turkey hen
   (with liver), 2.5-3 Kg
   (5 ¹/₂-7 lb)
Minced lean pork,
   150 g (5-6 oz)
3 pork sausages
Lard (sliced), 100 g (4 oz)
1 onion
1 rib of celery
1 cooking apple
Dried apricots and prunes
   (pitted), 100 g
   (4 oz; ¹/₂ cup)
Malaga sultanas,
   20 g (³/₄ oz; 1 tbsp)
Pine nuts,
   20 g (³/₄ oz; 1 tbsp)
8 large chestnuts
Bouquet garni, tied
   (bay leaf, oregano,
   rosemary, thyme)
Cinnamon powder
Fine dry breadcrumbs,
   30 g (1 oz; ¹/₄ cup)
1 lemon
Dry white wine
Salt and pepper
Cooking fat,
   30 g (1 oz; 2 tbsp)

Serves: 8-10	
Preparation: 30'+30'	
Cooking: 2h30'	
Difficulty: ● ● ●	
Flavour: ● ● ●	
Kcal (per serving): 938	
Proteins (per serving): 62	
Fats (per serving): 51	
Nutritional value: ● ● ●	

1 Half an hour before starting to prepare the stuffing, soak the apricots, prunes and sultanas in cold water. Score the skins of the chestnuts and roast them under the grill of the oven; when ready, remove the skins. Rinse and trim the vegetables; remove the peel and core of the apple. Rinse the herbs for the bouquet garni and tie them together. As far as the turkey is concerned, this should be ready for use: plucked and drawn, head and feet removed, passed over a flame to eliminate all residual quills, rinsed and dried. Rub the juice of the lemon both inside and over the outside of the bird, sprinkle a little salt over it and leave to one side.

2 Gently sauté the turkey liver for five minutes in a casserole containing the melted cooking fat, turning it over when the first side is cooked; remove the cooked liver and chop it up fine (2-3 chicken livers can be used as an alternative). Sauté the chopped onion and celery in the fat left in the casserole; add the crumbled sausages and the pork and brown slowly for about ten minutes.

3 Add the chopped liver, cubed apple, ground chestnuts, the drained and chopped apricots and prunes, the sultanas squeezed of all water, the pine nuts, a pinch of cinnamon, salt and pepper. Add the breadcrumbs and stir to mix. Pour half a glass of wine over the ingredients and allow the mixture to thicken for about ten minutes.

4 Stuff the turkey with the mixture and sew the belly with kitchen twine. Cover the bird with the slices of lard then bind it tightly with twine to keep it in shape. Put the turkey in an ovenproof dish together with the bouquet garni and cook it in the oven, preheated to 180°C (350°F), for approximately two hours, basting it every now and then with wine. When cooked, remove it from the oven, eliminate the twine and put the bird on a serving platter; arrange the lard all around it and serve, ready for carving.

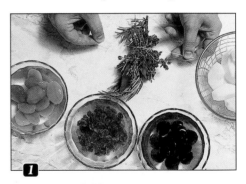

POLLO EN *SAMFAINA*

Chicken with aubergines and sweet peppers

1 chicken, ready for use, approx. 1.2 Kg (2 ¾ lb)
2 aubergines
2 sweet peppers
1 gourgette
1 onion
3 cloves of garlic
2 ripe tomatoes
Bay leaf, parsley and thyme
Dry white wine
Salt and pepper
Lard, 40 g (1 ½ oz)

Serves:	4-6
Preparation:	20'+30'
Cooking:	50'
Difficulty:	●●
Flavour:	●●
Kcal (per serving):	733
Proteins (per serving):	44
Fats (per serving):	49
Nutritional value:	●●

1 Half an hour before starting the meal, peel and slice the aubergines and put them in a bowl; cover them with salt, and weigh them down with a heavy object so that their bitter flavour 'sweats' out. In the meantime, clean and prepare the peppers and the gourgette. The chicken must be ready for use (plucked, entrails removed, passed over a flame to eliminate residual quills, rinsed and dried); cut it into 10-12 pieces, rub these with salt and pepper and leave to stand for 15 minutes.

2 Rinse the slices of aubergines, dry them well, cut them into cubes and stir-fry them for a couple of minutes in a casserole with a tablespoon of melted lard; add the roughly cut peppers and the diced gourgette and allow the flavours to blend.

3 Melt the remaining lard in another casserole (earthenware this time) and brown the chicken pieces in it with the thinly sliced onion. Add the chopped garlic and tomatoes; stir over intense heat for 2-3 minutes then add a glass (not full) of wine, a bay leaf, a sprig each of thyme and parsley, salt and pepper. Lower the heat to minimum, cover the casserole and simmer very gently for about half an hour.

4 At the end of this time, take the lid off, increase the heat to medium, add the aubergines, peppers and gourgette and reduce the liquid for about ten minutes. Serve immediately.

1 chicken, ready for use,
  1.2 Kg (2 $\frac{1}{2}$ lbs)
1 onion
8-10 (according to size)
  fresh green peppers
  (small, oblong type)
3 cloves of garlic
Fresh oregano
Grated nutmeg
1 clove
Dry white wine
1 lemon
Salt and pepper
Cooking fat,
  30 g (1 $\frac{1}{4}$ oz; 2 tbsp)

Serves: 4
Preparation: 20'
Cooking: 40'
Difficulty: ● ●
Flavour: ● ● ●
Kcal (per serving): 715
Proteins (per serving): 44
Fats (per serving): 49
Nutritional value: ● ● ●

POLLO CON PIMIENTOS

Chicken with small green peppers ◀

Peel the onion and the cloves of garlic and chop them fine. Prepare the peppers by removing the stalks, seeds and fibrous parts, and cutting them into strips (or in half if they are small). The chicken must be already plucked and drawn, passed over a flame to remove any residual quills, rinsed and dried; cut it into approximately twelve pieces. Gently brown the chicken pieces in the cooking fat in a casserole (preferably earthenware with a lid), turning them over frequently to brown them evenly on all sides. Add the chopped garlic and onion, season with salt and pepper, a pinch of grated nutmeg, the crushed clove, the leaves from a sprig of fresh oregano, and three quarters of a glass of wine. Cover the casserole, bring to the boil and simmer for 15 minutes; thereafter, add the peppers and the juice of the lemon, put the lid back on and simmer for a further 15 minutes (check that the chicken is cooked before removing from the heat; a further 5-6 minutes may be necessary).
Serve immediately together with the peppers.

PERDICES CON COLES

Partridges in cabbage parcels

Rinse and trim the vegetables and herbs according to their use. The partridge meat should be sufficiently hung, then the fowl must be plucked, entrails removed, passed over a flame to eliminate residual quills, rinsed and dried (if the partridges are small then three will be required). Cut them into two lengthwise and season them inside and out with salt, pepper, and a pinch each of powdered cinnamon and grated nutmeg. Brown them, turning them over every now and then, in a casserole with 2-3 tablespoons of oil, the lard cut into strips and the roughly chopped onion and carrot. After about ten minutes, add the bouquet garni, half a glass of wine and a ladle of hot broth; cover the casserole with its lid and bring to the boil. Lower the heat and simmer for about one hour. In the meantime, blanch the cabbage (unsliced) for 5-6 minutes in slightly salted boiling water; drain it then very gently separate the leaves. Select the largest and best-shaped leaves, spreading them out on a cutting board and taking care to not damage them; these will be used to wrap each half partridge, which should be tender by now. Wrap the leaves tightly round the partridges, briefly dip the 'parcels' in the beaten eggs, then in the flour; arrange them in an ovenproof dish with a lid, basting them with their gravy diluted with a little broth. Add the sliced *butifarra*, place the lid on the casserole and put in the oven pre-heated to 180°C/350°F for 30 minutes. If partridges are unavailable, quails may be used (one or two per person, depending upon their size).

2 large partridges, ready for cooking, approx. 1.2 Kg (2 1/2 lbs each)
Lard, 70 g (3 oz)
Butifarra blanca (see page 22), 100 g (4 oz)
Half a cabbage, 1 onion
Half a carrot
Bouquet garni, tied (bay leaf, oregano and thyme)
Red wine
Chicken or beef broth (ready-made), approx. 2 litres (3 1/2 pints)
2 eggs
Plain flour, 20 g (3/4 oz; 1 1/2 tbsp)
Powdered cinnamon and grated nutmeg
Salt and pepper
Olive oil

Serves:	4
Preparation:	20'
Cooking:	1h45'
Difficulty:	● ● ●
Flavour:	● ●
Kcal (per serving):	559
Proteins (per serving):	50
Fats (per serving):	34
Nutritional value:	● ●

MAR I TERRA

Chicken with lobster and chocolate

1 chicken (with liver),
  approx. 1.2 Kg (2 ½ lb)
1 lobster (or crawfish),
  approx. 1 Kg (2 lb 2 oz)
1 onion
2-3 ripe tomatoes
2 cloves of garlic
A piece of leek
Shelled and peeled almonds
  and hazelnuts
  (a small handful)
Bouquet garni, tied
  (bay leaf, oregano,
  parsley, thyme) plus an
  extra sprig of parsley
Peel of half an orange
Cinnamon and saffron
Dark chocolate
  (or unsweetened cocoa),
  20 g (1 oz)
Dry white wine
Dry breadcrumbs
Salt and pepper
Olive oil

Serves:	6-8
Preparation:	20'
Cooking:	45'+10'
Difficulty:	●●
Flavour:	●●
Kcal (per serving):	673
Proteins (per serving):	46
Fats (per serving):	40
Nutritional value:	●●●

1 Toast the almonds and hazelnuts for about ten minutes in the oven pre-heated to 200°C (375°F). As usual, the chicken must be ready for use (plucked, entrails removed, passed over a flame to eliminate residual quills, rinsed and dried); cut it into small pieces and rub these with a mixture of salt, pepper and a pinch of cinnamon, shaking off the excess. Brown the chicken pieces and the cleaned liver in an earthenware casserole (with lid) until golden-brown.

2 Remove the liver and add the chopped onion and leek; allow these to stew slowly then add the bouquet garni, the grated orange peel, the rinsed and chopped tomatoes (without seeds), and two glasses of wine. Lower the heat under the casserole and gently simmer until the liquid has reduced to half its volume (about 15 minutes); add two tablespoons of breadcrumbs, sufficient hot water to cover the pieces of chicken, put the lid on the casserole and gently simmer for a further 15 minutes.

3 In the meantime, pound in a mortar (or in a food mixer) the almonds, hazelnuts, garlic, chicken liver and the crumbled chocolate; add a pinch of saffron to this paste and dilute it with a drop of hot water.

4 Rinse and prepare the lobster: remove the shell and cut the flesh into 8-10 pieces (not too thick) and briefly fry in a little oil in a pan, then add to the chicken in the casserole. Add the paste from the mortar and mix gently to combine all the flavours; remove from the heat. After a few minutes, eliminate the bouquet garni, sprinkle with chopped parsley and serve.

Barcelona, Palau del Mar,
site of the Catalonia History Museum.

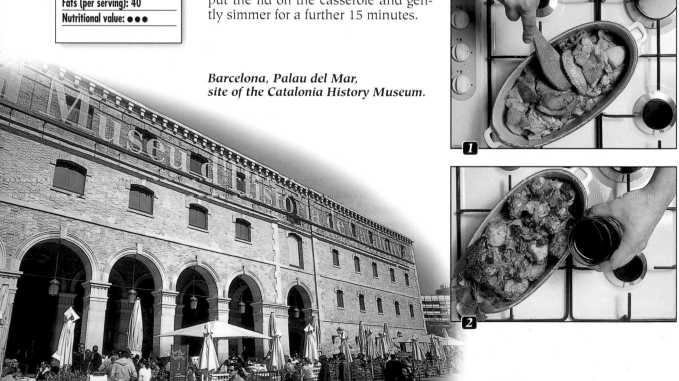

PORC AMB MUSCLOS

Pork with mussels

Lean pork, 500 g (1 lb 2 oz)	
Fresh mussels, approx. 900 g (2 lbs)	
1 onion	
4 ripe tomatoes	
3 cloves of garlic	
Mild pimiento powder (*pimentón dulce*)	
1 dry red pimiento	
Bay leaf	
Parsley	
Lemon rind (a strip)	
Dry white wine	
Salt and pepper	
Olive oil	

Serves: 4	
Preparation: 20'	
Cooking: 1h	
Difficulty: ●●	
Flavour: ●●●	
Kcal (per serving): 405	
Proteins (per serving): 34	
Fats (per serving): 19	
Nutritional value: ●●	

Prepare the mussels by scraping the shells, pulling the 'beards' out, and then rinsing them well. Rinse and trim the vegetables and herbs according to their use. Cut the pork into bite-size pieces and brown them slowly in a pan with a little oil; keep in a warm place. Gently sauté the chopped onion and the peeled and crushed cloves of garlic in a casserole with 4-5 tablespoons of oil; add the diced tomatoes, a teaspoon of *pimentón*, a bay leaf, the strip of lemon rind and the dry pimiento (without seeds). Cover the casserole and simmer for about 20 minutes.

In the meantime, put the mussels in a pan with sufficient water to barely cover them, a glass of wine (not full) and a sprig of parsley. Put the lid on the casserole and allow the valves to open over medium heat; remove from the stove and, eliminating any mussels that have failed to open, discard the empty part of the shells leaving the flesh in the other halves. Filter the mussel cooking liquid into the casserole, add the pork mixture, put the lid back on and simmer for about 30 minutes, tasting for salt and pepper. Shortly before the end of the cooking time, add the mussels in their half shells and, without putting the lid on the casserole, let everything heat through. This recipe, like the previous one, is a blend of the sea and the land, the Mediterranean and Catalonia (or, to be precise, *Mar i Muntanya*).

An inlet along the Costa Brava coast, a popular tourist area.

FISH, SHELLFISH AND SEAFOOD

*Fish, seafood and lobsters freshly caught
in the waters of Costa Brava:
how can all this goodness be used to the best?
In simple and sometimes elaborate recipes
for appetising second courses
or for all-in-one dishes like the rich suquet.
Even land snails are given rightful importance
in Catalonia, where they are cooked
in a variety of manners.*

4

CAP ROIG CON SALSA DE AJO

Garlic scorpion fish ▶

1 scorpion fish,
  approx. 1.2 Kg (2 1/2 lb)
3-4 cloves of garlic
Fish broth
  (made with bouillon cubes)
Parsley (large sprig)
Dry white wine
Salt
Olive oil

Serves: 4

Preparation: 10'+30'

Cooking: 30'

Difficulty: ●

Flavour: ●●

Kcal (per serving): 347

Proteins (per serving): 38

Fats (per serving): 15

Nutritional value: ●

Prepare the fish by removing the scales (be careful with the sharp fins) and the entrails, then rinse it well inside and out. Rub it all over with salt and leave to stand for about 30 minutes; thereafter, place it in an oiled oven-proof dish and pour a glass of fish broth and half a glass of wine over it. Cook in the oven pre-heated to 180°C (350°F) for just under 30 minutes. Peel the garlic cloves and slice them lengthwise, then fry them until golden in a small pot with half a glass of oil. Remove from the heat, add the chopped parsley. Drain the fish and serve it with the aromatic sauce and slices of lemon.

10 dozen land snails,
  purged and rinsed
1 onion
4 cloves of garlic
Sprigs of wild fennel
Sprigs of fresh mint, parsley
  and thyme
Caraway seeds
1 clove
1 dry red pimiento
Salt, peppercorns
Alioli sauce,
  for accompaniment
  (see page 72)

Serves: 4

Preparation: 15'

Cooking: 1h50'

Difficulty: ●

Flavour: ●●

Kcal (per serving): 249

Proteins (per serving): 29

Fats (per serving): 13

Nutritional value: ●

CARACOLES A LA PATARRALLADA

Grilled snails

The snails should be ready for use: purged to expel all impurities, foam and slime, and rinsed well. Blanch them in plenty of boiling water for five minutes then drain. Peel the onion and garlic and rinse the herbs. Fill a pot to three-quarters full with cold water, add the sliced onion, the cloves of garlic, a pinch of salt, 4-5 peppercorns, a small pinch of caraway seeds, the clove, the pimiento, a few sprigs of parsley and wild fennel, and some mint and thyme leaves. Bring to the boil then add the snails, lower the heat to minimum, put the lid on and simmer for one and a half hours. In the meantime, prepare the embers in the barbecue or grill (the charcoal or wood should be glowing, without flames). When the snails are ready, drain them thoroughly then cook them on the grill (or under the grill of an oven) with their cavities topmost for about ten minutes. Serve them in their shells (provide toothpicks or the specific utensils for extracting the flesh) together with plenty of *alioli* as a dip. Cooked this way (the recipe is often used for sea-winkles as well) the snails can be served as *hors d'œuvre* or with other *tapas*.

DORADA A LA SAL

Gilthead in salt ◄

1 gilthead,
   approx. 1 Kg (2 lbs)
Coarse salt,
   as much as needed
Alioli sauce,
   for accompaniment
   (see page 72)

Serves: 4
Preparation: 10'
Cooking: 2h30'
Difficulty: ●
Flavour: ● ●
Kcal (per serving): 250
Proteins (per serving): 34
Fats (per serving): 12
Nutritional value: ●

This method of cooking goes back through the centuries and leaves the meat (or fish) tasty, moist and fragrant. Prepare the gilthead: gut it, then rinse and dry it. Cover the bottom of an ovenproof dish (preferably earthenware) with a three-quarters of an inch layer of coarse salt. Place the fish on top of this, but do not add any other seasoning. Cover it completely with more salt, making sure that the top layer is at least three-quarters of an inch thick. Put the dish in the oven, preheated to 160°C (320°F), and cook for two and a half hours; at this point the salt should be a solid block with a golden-brown crust. Crack the crust open, remove the fish and eliminate all traces of excess salt before serving; accompany it with plenty of *alioli* sauce in a separate dish.

CARACOLES *A LA LLAUNA*

Snails au gratin

Rinse and trim the vegetables and herbs according to their use. The snails should have been boiled previously according to the instructions given in the recipe on page 60 (*Caracoles a la patarrallada*), extracted from their shells and kept in a warm place. Prepare the *sofrito*: finely chop the onion together with the lard, garlic and parsley, and sauté slowly in a pan with 3-4 tablespoons of oil. Add the diced tomatoes and the sugar, stir and allow the flavours to blend very slowly. Slice the two types of *butifarra* into rounds; add them to the other ingredients in the pan and mix to combine the flavours. Remove from the stove and keep in a warm place.

Finely chop the other three cloves of garlic and sauté gently for a few minutes in a casserole (or ovenproof dish) in 3 tablespoons of oil, season with salt and pepper and a teaspoon of *pimentón*; add the drained snails and toss-fry for five minutes over intense heat. Ladle the *sofrito* and rounds of *butifarra* over the snails and place the casserole in a medium oven for 15 minutes, until the surface becomes golden. Serve immediately.

Land snails, boiled
   and shelled (see above),
   300 g (10 oz)
3 cloves of garlic
Bay leaf
Mild pimiento powder
   (*pimentón dulce*)

Salt
Olive oil

For the sofrito
Lard, 100 g (4 oz)
Butifarra blanca (see page
   22), 200 g (2 oz)

Butifarra negra (see page
   22), 200 g (2 oz)
1 onion
3 cloves of garlic
2-3 ripe tomatoes
Parsley
Castor sugar, 5 g (1 tsp)

Serves: 4
Preparation: 20'
Cooking: 40'
Difficulty: ● ●
Flavour: ● ● ●
Kcal (per serving): 419
Proteins (per serving): 12

Fats (per serving): 36
Nutritional value: ● ● ●

JIBIAS CON SETAS

Cuttlefish with mushrooms

Cuttlefish, 1 Kg (2 lb 2 oz)
Boletus (or chanterelle) mushrooms, 500 g (1 lb 2 oz)
2 onions
5 cloves of garlic
Tomato pulp, 2.5 dl (6 fl oz)
Shelled, toasted almonds, approx. 12
1 fresh red pimiento
Dry white wine
Salt
Olive oil

Serves:	4
Preparation:	25'
Cooking:	1h 10'
Difficulty:	●●
Flavour:	●●
Kcal (per serving):	397
Proteins (per serving):	42
Fats (per serving):	14
Nutritional value:	●

1 Prepare the cuttlefish: eliminate the cuttlebone, entrails, eyes and 'beaks', and the ink sacs. Rinse them well inside and out, remove the outside membrane then cut the bodies into strips. Peel the onions, cut them into thick slices and fry until golden in a casserole (preferably earthenware) with 6-8 tablespoons of oil; add the tomato pulp and the pimiento (left whole) and simmer slowly for about 10 minutes to blend all the flavours. Add the cuttlefish, and salt to taste, then cover with hot water. Put the lid on the casserole and simmer for about 30 minutes.

2 In the meantime, prepare the mushrooms by gently scraping off the soil and wiping them with a piece of damp kitchen paper (do not rinse them); cut them into small pieces, add to the cuttlefish, then continue to cook for a further 15 minutes.

3 Toast the almonds in the oven then pound them in a mortar together with the peeled garlic; dilute the paste obtained with half a glass of wine. Add this mixture to the cuttlefish and mushrooms cooking in the casserole, stir, taste for salt, put the lid back on and finish cooking (about another 10 minutes). Serve immediately.

Ancient Roman remains in Catalonia.

2 medium-sized lobsters
1 onion
Bouquet garni, tied
  (bay leaf, parsley,
  thyme and a few strips
  of lemon rind)
Dry white wine
Lettuce leaves
  (for serving)
Salt
Olive oil

For the picada
Almond kernels,
  50 g (2 oz; $^1/_4$ cup)
1 sachet of saffron powder
1 clove of garlic
Ground mild pimiento
  (*pimentón dulce*)
1 fresh red pimiento
Parsley
Dry breadcrumbs,
  10 g ($^1/_2$ oz; $^3/_4$ tbsp)
Dark chocolate,
  50 g (2 oz) in one piece
Dry white wine

Serves: 4	
Preparation: 20'	
Cooking: 35'	
Difficulty: ●●	
Flavour: ●●●	
Kcal (per serving): 428	
Proteins (per serving): 23	
Fats (per serving): 25	
Nutritional value: ●●	

The picada is a tasty gravy for cooking meat, fish and vegetables and the ingredients can vary according to the dish (almonds, however, are always present); sometimes it actually looks like and can be used as a sauce.

LANGOSTA A LA COSTA BRAVA

Lobster in chocolate-flavoured *picada*

First of all, prepare the *picada*: toast the almonds in the oven, peel them then grind them to a paste in a mortar (or blender) with the peeled garlic, the chocolate broken into pieces, a sprig of parsley and the red pimiento without its seeds. Put the paste in a bowl and add the saffron, a couple of teaspoons of ground pimiento, the breadcrumbs and a drop of wine; mix the *picada* well and leave to one side.

Rinse the lobsters, cut them in two lengthwise, eliminate the intestinal tract, extract the flesh and cut it into pieces about 2 cm ($^3/_4$ inch) long. Peel and finely chop the onion then sauté it in a pan with 4-5 tablespoons of oil; add the bouquet garni, the pieces of lobster and a pinch of salt; toss fry over intense heat for 2-3 minutes. Lower the heat, add the prepared *picada*, mix well to allow the flavours to blend and taste for salt; put the lid on the pan and simmer for fifteen minutes, adding a few tablespoons of hot water if the gravy reduces too much. Remove the bouquet garni and serve the lobster on a bed of lettuce leaves.

ANGUILA AL *ALLI I PEBRE*

Stewed eels

Slit the eels open to remove the entrails, eliminate the heads and fins (skin them only if they are too big), rinse them well then cut them into 6-8 cm/3 inch slices; season the pieces with salt and pepper. Slowly heat 4-5 tablespoons of oil in a casserole (preferably earthenware); add a tablespoon of *pimentón* diluted with a little broth to flavour the oil without allowing it to overheat. Add the rest of the broth, bring to the boil, put the lid on the casse-role, lower the flame and simmer for 15 minutes. To make the *pica-da*, toast the almonds in the oven, peel them then pound them in a mortar (or food proces-sor) together with the garlic, saf-fron and a sprig of parsley to ob-tain a paste; blend the paste with a little of the broth simmering in the casserole and season with salt and pepper. When the broth is ready, add the pieces of eel to it, then the *picada*; put the lid back on and cook until tender. Uncover, briefly reduce the liquid and serve the stewed eels gar-nished with sprigs of parsley.

Medium-sized eels, ready
  for use, 1 Kg (2 lbs 2 oz)
Mild pimiento powder
  (*pimentón dulce*)
Vegetable broth
  (ready made),
  approx. 1 litre (2 pints)
Parsley (for garnish)
Salt and pepper
Olive oil

For the picada
Shelled almonds,
  70 g (3 oz)
1 sachet of saffron powder
2 cloves of garlic
Parsley

Serves:	4
Preparation:	20'
Cooking:	45'
Difficulty:	● ●
Flavour:	● ● ●
Kcal (per serving):	804
Proteins (per serving):	40
Fats (per serving):	68
Nutritional value:	● ● ●

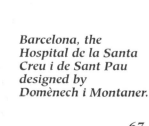

Barcelona, the Hospital de la Santa Creu i de Sant Pau designed by Domènech i Montaner.

PATACO

Fresh tuna with clams and vegetables ▶

1 slice of fresh tuna,
    approx. 700 g (1 ½ lbs)
30 (approx.) large clams
1 onion
2 ripe cooking tomatoes
1 potato
1 gourgette
Parsley
Red wine
Salt
Olive oil

For the picada
Shelled almonds,
    50 g (2 oz; 2 tbsp)
1 sachet of saffron powder
2 cloves of garlic
Mild ground pimiento
    (*pimentón dulce*)
Parsley

Serves:	4
Preparation:	25'+2h
Cooking:	40'
Difficulty:	● ●
Flavour:	● ● ●
Kcal (per serving):	425
Proteins (per serving):	45
Fats (per serving):	13
Nutritional value:	● ●

1 Prior to starting the dish, soak the clams at length in cold water (changing it twice) to eliminate all traces of sand and impurities. Soak the tuna in cold water to let it 'bleed'. Blanch the almonds in boiling water for ten minutes then drain, dry and peel them and put to one side. Rinse and prepare all the vegetables according to their use. Finely chop the onion and sauté it slowly in a casserole (preferably earthenware with a lid) with 5-6 tablespoons of oil for 3-4 minutes; add the roughly chopped tomatoes and gently stew for five minutes. Add the diced potato and gourgette, half a glass of wine and sufficient water to cover the ingredients. Put the lid on the casserole, bring to the boil, then lower the heat and simmer for about fifteen minutes.

2 Drain the tuna, dry it then cut it into thin strips; add these to the casserole together with the rinsed clams and a pinch of salt. Put the lid back on and simmer for a further ten minutes. In the meantime, prepare the *picada*: grind the almonds to a paste in a mortar (or blender) with the peeled garlic and a sprig of parsley; put the paste obtained into a bowl and add the saffron, a couple of teaspoons of ground pimiento, a drop of the cooking liquid from the pan and mix well. Add this *picada* to the casserole when the fish is cooked and allow the flavours to blend. Eliminate any clams that have failed to open, then serve the tuna immediately together with the clams in their shells, garnishing the dish with sprigs of parsley. Instead of clams in the *pataco*, sea-winkles may be used, cooking and flavouring them separately (as described on page 60) and removing the flesh from the shells.

ESQUEIXADA DE BACALAO

Dried codfish salad

Soaked codfish,
    600 g (1 ¼ lb)
1 onion
2 sweet peppers
3-4 salad tomatoes
3 spring onions
2 cloves of garlic, chopped
Green and black olives
    in brine (for garnish)
Vinegar
Salt and pepper
Olive oil

Serves:	4
Preparation:	20'
Cooking:	5-6' (optional)
Difficulty:	●
Flavour:	● ●
Kcal (per serving):	337
Proteins (per serving):	35
Fats (per serving):	17
Nutritional value:	●

This fish salad is delicious served cold in warm weather. The soaked and skinned codfish is usually used raw, but if preferred it can be blanched briefly in unsalted boiling water then drained well. Rinse and trim the vegetables according to their use, eliminating all skins, seeds and tough parts. Cut the onion into thin slices and soak them in slightly salted cold water for about ten minutes to remove the pungent taste. Flake the codfish by hand into a salad bowl; add the drained onion, the finely sliced sweet peppers and the diced tomatoes. Cut the spring onions crosswise into rings and arrange on top of the other ingredients, together with the chopped garlic, then season with oil, vinegar, salt and pepper. Decorate with the olives and serve (in the height of Summer, keep in the fridge for two hours before serving). Another excellent salad made with dried codfish, *empedrat*, which is more suited for Autumn, foresees the addition of boiled haricot beans and hard-boiled eggs.

RAPE EN SALSA DE ALMENDRAS

Anglerfish in almond sauce

Anglerfish (in slices),
  800 g (1 ³/₄ lb)
1 onion
2 cloves of garlic
1 slice of farmhouse bread
  (without crust)
Peeled almonds (two dozen)
Parsley
1 sachet of saffron powder
Plain flour,
  approx. 40 g (4 tbsp)
Fish broth (made from
  bouillon cubes)
Dry white wine
Salt and pepper
Olive oil

Serves: 4	
Preparation: 15'	
Cooking: 30'	
Difficulty: ●●	
Flavour: ●●	
Kcal (per serving): 478	
Proteins (per serving): 38	
Fats (per serving): 19	
Nutritional value: ●	

1 Blanch the almonds for about 4-5 minutes in boiling water without salt; drain, remove the skins then dry them. Dip the slices of fish into the flour, coating both sides and shaking them to eliminate any excess flour. Brown them (one or two at a time if they are big) on both sides in a pan with 6 tablespoons of oil; drain them and put them into an ovenproof dish.

2 Using the oil left in the pan, slowly sauté the almonds, the bread cut into small cubes, and the peeled cloves of garlic, until the latter are pale gold. Pour everything in the pan into a food mixer and grind to a fine paste with a sprig of parsley; transfer the paste to a bowl, stir in the saffron and dilute with half a glass of wine.

3 Sauté the chopped onion in the oil left in the pan (add more fresh oil if necessary); add the almond paste and mix well, stirring gently over low heat for 5-6 minutes.

4 Add one dl/4 fl oz of fish broth (or even hot water), mix and add salt and pepper to taste. Pour this sauce over the fish slices and bake in the oven, preheated to 180°C (350°F) for 15 minutes. Serve immediately.

SUQUET DE PESCADO CON ALIOLI

Mixed fish casserole with *alioli* sauce

1 First of all, prepare the *picada:* toast the almonds in the oven, peel them then pound them in a mortar (or food processor) together with the peeled garlic; put the resulting paste in a bowl and mix with the saffron, a couple of teaspoons of ground pimiento, a pinch each of ground cinnamon and salt, and the breadcrumbs. Stir well with a drop of wine and leave to stand.

2 Next, make the *alioli* sauce, the famous garlic mayonnaise that is used in recipes as far afield as Provence. Pound the peeled garlic in a mortar with a pinch of salt to obtain a paste; put this in a bowl and gently add (stirring all the time with a wooden spoon) the egg yolk and the juice of the lemon. Still stirring in the same direction, very slowly add the oil, drop after drop, until the sauce becomes thick and creamy (this can also be done with an electric blender but less oil will be needed). Put the *alioli* in the fridge (the doses indicated here are sufficient for four persons).

3 The fish should be already rinsed and trimmed, according to use, just like the vegetables. Chop the onion and the clove of garlic with a sprig of parsley; slowly sauté this mixture in 3-4 tablespoons of oil in a casserole (preferably earthenware with a lid). Add the roughly chopped tomatoes, half a glass of wine, salt and pepper; allow the flavours to mix for five minutes then add the potatoes peeled and sliced into rounds and a bay leaf. Pour in sufficient hot water to cover the ingredients, bring to the boil and cook over intense heat for fifteen minutes.

4 Add the fish cut into pieces, another half glass of wine and sufficient hot water to make up the volume of that evaporated during cooking in the previous step. Bring to the boil, add the carefully rinsed whole prawns (or scampi), lower the heat, cover the casserole and simmer for ten minutes. Thereafter, add the *picada* and mix over gentle heat. Remove the casserole from the stove, and add a couple of tablespoons of *alioli* to the broth. Serve the remaining *alioli* in a sauce boat placed next to the *suquet* on the table so that each guest can help himself.

Mixed fish for stewing
(frog fish or angler fish,
conger-eel, codfish, smooth
hound, red mullet,
gurnard, etc.),
800 g (1 3/4 lbs)
12 king prawns (or scampi)
5 medium-sized potatoes
1 onion
1 clove of garlic
2-3 ripe cooking tomatoes
Bay leaf, parsley
Dry white wine
Salt and pepper
Olive oil

For the picada
Almond kernels,
50 g (2 oz; 2 tbsp)
1 sachet of saffron powder
1 clove of garlic
Ground mild pimiento
(*pimentón dulce*)
Ground cinnamon
Dry breadcrumbs,
10 g (1/2 oz; 3/4 tbsp)
Dry white wine
Salt

For the alioli *sauce*
1 egg yolk
4 cloves of garlic
Half a lemon
Salt
Olive oil, 2.5 dl (1/2 pint)

Serves:	4
Preparation:	30'
Cooking:	40'
Difficulty:	●●●
Flavour:	●●●
Kcal (per serving):	1315
Proteins (per serving):	50
Fats (per serving):	86
Nutritional value:	●●●

MEJILLONES RELLENOS

Stuffed mussels

Mussels, 1 Kg (2 ¹/₄ lb)
2 sweet peppers
1 onion
1 clove of garlic
Parsley
Dry white wine
Salt and pepper
Olive oil

Serves:	4
Preparation:	25'
Cooking:	20'
Difficulty:	●
Flavour:	● ●
Kcal (per serving):	273
Proteins (per serving):	19
Fats (per serving):	13
Nutritional value:	●

S crape the shells of the mussels, remove the 'whiskers' between the valves, and rinse them well but do not dry them. Rinse the peppers, remove the stalks, seeds and fibrous parts; cut the peppers into strips or dice them then stew them slowly for 3-4 minutes in a pan, with the sliced garlic and onion and 3-4 tablespoons of oil.
Add the mussels, a glass of wine and a few sprigs of parsley.
Cover the pan and cook for about ten minutes, until all the mussels have opened.
Remove the pan from the heat; extract the mussels and place them on a serving dish, discarding the empty shell of each one.
Filter the liquid left in the pan; distribute spoonfuls of the ingredients left in the sieve into the mussels in the half shells then pour some of the filtered liquid over them, add a pinch of salt and if desired, a dash of freshly ground pepper.
Serve the mussels at room temperature, sprinkled with chopped parsley. This is a simple dish that is ideal in Summer, but it can also be used as a tasty appetiser, served with an excellent dry white wine brought up from the cellar.

Eggs
and
VEGETABLES

*In line with a cuisine that enjoys combing ingredients
and flavours, even many of the recipes
for vegetables can provide all-in-one dishes
– with the addition of* alioli, samfaina *and* sofrito –
rather than just serve as accompaniments.
Escalivada *is but one example of this.*

5

BERENJENAS A LA CATALANA

Aubergines with walnuts

3 aubergines
Kernels of 6-7 walnuts
1 onion
2 cloves of garlic
2 tomatoes
Parsley
A small amount
of vegetable broth
(made from bouillon
cubes)
Salt and pepper
Olive oil

Serves: 4	
Preparation: 15'+30'	
Cooking: 30'	
Difficulty: ●●	
Flavour: ●●	
Kcal (per serving): 256	
Proteins (per serving): 7	
Fats (per serving): 20	
Nutritional value: ●●	

1 Peel the aubergines and cut them into slices, putting them on a plate; cover the slices with salt and weigh them down with a heavy object for about 30 minutes to allow the bitterness to 'sweat out'.

2 Toss-fry the walnut kernels in a casserole with 5 tablespoons of oil; remove them with a draining spoon and leave to drain on kitchen paper. Rinse and dry the aubergine slices and cut them into small cubes; fry them for 2-3 minutes over intense heat in the oil left in the casserole, then add the peeled and chopped onion and garlic.

3 Mix well and cook for a further 2-3 minutes; lower the heat and add the rinsed and diced tomatoes (without seeds).

4 Pound the walnuts to a paste in a mortar (or food processor) and dilute with half a glass of lukewarm vegetable broth. Pour this mixture into the casserole and season with salt and pepper. Simmer slowly until the aubergines are tender. Serve sprinkled with chopped parsley.

SBA-4-4225

COLES A LA CATALANA

Cabbage in spicy sauce ◄

Prepare the *romesco* sauce well beforehand, using the recipe on page 14 and leaving it to stand at room temperature. Prepare the cabbage, eliminating the core and the thickest outer leaves, and blanch it in plenty of slightly salted boiling water; drain, slice into shreds and put these in a casserole (preferably earthenware) together with the *romesco* sauce. Simmer slowly over very low heat for about ten minutes, stirring gently and tasting for salt. Remove the casserole from the stove, put its lid on and leave to cool. Once cool, leave to stand for another hour. Shortly before taking the casserole to the table, put it briefly on the stove, uncovered, to warm up the ingredients.

This is an excellent accompaniment for pork dishes and is even delicious when made with cauliflower.

A good-sized cabbage
Romesco sauce
  (see page 14, recipe for
  Gambas en salsa romesco)
Salt

Serves: 4
Preparation: 25'+1h
Cooking: 25'
Difficulty: ● ●
Flavour: ● ● ●
Kcal (per serving): 236
Proteins (per serving): 3
Fats (per serving): 15
Nutritional value: ● ●

ESPINACAS A LA CATALANA

Catalan-style spinach

Soak the sultanas in cold water for 30' before starting to prepare the dish. Trim the spinach leaves and rinse them several times under cold running water. Without draining them, put them into a pot to blanch, using only the water attached to the leaves (or only a little more) and a pinch of salt; drain them, squeeze them with your hands to remove as much liquid as possible, then chop them fine. Sauté the peeled garlic in a pan with 4 tablespoons of oil; as soon as the garlic starts to colour, remove it and add the spinach, pinenuts and sultanas (squeezed of all water) to the pan. Allow the flavours to blend over medium heat, stirring frequently. This is an excellent accompaniment for meat dishes; if two anchovies in oil, a hard-boiled egg are added, it becomes a delicious meal.

Fresh spinach,
  approx. 1 Kg (2 lbs 2 oz)
1 clove of garlic
Pine nuts,
  30 g (1 1/4 oz; 1 1/2 tbsp)
Sultanas,
  30 g (1 1/4 oz; 1 1/2 tbsp)
Olive oil

Serves: 4
Preparation: 20'+30'
Cooking: 15'
Difficulty: ●
Flavour: ● ● ●
Kcal (per serving): 529
Proteins (per serving): 78
Fats (per serving): 16
Nutritional value: ● ● ●

ESCALIVADA

Oven-baked vegetable salad

1 large aubergine
2 ripe tomatoes
2 sweet peppers
1 onion
Vinegar
Coarse salt
Olive oil

Serves: 4	
Preparation: 15′	
Cooking: 45′	
Difficulty: ●	
Flavour: ● ● ●	
Kcal (per serving): 139	
Proteins (per serving): 3	
Fats (per serving): 10	
Nutritional value: ● ●	

Rinse and trim the vegetables according to their use, but peel the onion only. Prepare sheets of tinfoil large enough to wrap the vegetables separately according to type (both tomatoes together, the onion on its own, etc.). Season the vegetables with salt and add a little oil before closing the little parcels;

place them on an oven rack and bake in the oven, preheated to 180°C/350°F, for about 45 minutes. Remove them from the oven and allow to cool before opening them. Peel the aubergine, then cut all the vegetables into thin strips; put in a salad bowl, dress with oil and vinegar and serve.

FAVES AL TOMBET

Broad beans with lettuce ▶

Fresh, podded broad
  or haricot beans, 700 g
  or 350 g if dry beans are
  used (1 lb 10 oz or 14 oz)
1 head of lettuce
2-3 cloves of garlic
1 slice of farmhouse bread
  (without crust)
Ground pimiento
Red wine vinegar
Vegetable broth
  (made with bouillon cubes)
Salt and pepper
Olive oil

Serves: 4	
Preparation: 15′+4h	
Cooking: 50′	
Difficulty: ● ●	
Flavour: ● ● ●	
Kcal (per serving): 214	
Proteins (per serving): 12	
Fats (per serving): 10	
Nutritional value: ● ●	

If dry beans are being used, soak them for 3-4 hours before starting to prepare this dish. Rinse and trim the lettuce, eliminate the core, and roughly chop it up.
Fry the slice of bread in a casserole (preferably earthenware) with the peeled garlic and 5-6 tablespoons of oil; drain both the bread and the garlic, pound them in a mortar (or food mixer) to obtain a paste, adding half a teaspoon of ground pimiento and a tablespoon of vinegar.
Drain the beans and slowly sauté them for about 15 minutes in the oil left in the casserole, together with the chopped lettuce; add the paste containing the bread, 2-3 ladles of broth, a pinch of salt and pepper. Cover the casserole and simmer for about 30 minutes. Serve immediately. This is excellent served with eggs or *tortillas*.

This recipe originally calls for fresh broad beans but it is equally delicious if made with other types of beans, like the large white Spanish butter beans. We have chosen this latter solution since the season for fresh butter beans is longer than that for broad beans; if dry varieties are used the dish can be made all year round. Nevertheless, when fresh broad beans are available these must be used.

ROVELLONS A LA BRASA

Grilled mushrooms

Boletus mushroom
   caps (medium-sized),
   500 g (1 lb 2 oz)
4 cloves of garlic
Parsley
Salt
Olive oil

Serves: 4	
Preparation: 15′	
Cooking: 15′	
Difficulty: ● ●	
Flavour: ● ● ●	
Kcal (per serving): 141	
Proteins (per serving): 6	
Fats (per serving): 10	
Nutritional value: ●	

Scrape the mushroom caps delicately with a small knife to eliminate all soil and impurities; wipe them gently with a damp (not wet) cloth then dry them with a kitchen towel or kitchen paper. If nursery-grown field mushrooms are being used – and this recipe is fine for them as well – they must be rinsed under cold running water and dried very carefully. Peel and finely chop the garlic together with a generous sprig of parsley. Lightly oil the underside of the mushroom caps, place them upside down on the grill and cook over glowing coals (or under the grill of the oven) without turning them over. When ready, transfer them to a serving platter, sprinkle with a little salt and the chopped garlic and parsley; drizzle some raw oil over the prepared mushrooms and serve.

Barcelona, Museum of Contemporary Art.

HABAS A LA CATALANA

Broad beans with mixed cured meats

If dried beans are being used, these will have to be soaked for 5-6 hours before starting the recipe. Cut the lard into strips and fry it in the melted cooking fat in a casserole (preferably earthenware with a lid); add the peeled and chopped onion and garlic, sauté them until they begin to colour, then add the drained beans and the two types of *butifarra*; simmer slowly all together. In the meantime, pound a pinch of *matalahúva* (aniseed) and a small stick of cinnamon in a mortar;

add these to the beans in the pot along with a pinch each of salt and pepper, the bouquet garni, two full glasses of wine and sufficient hot water to completely cover the ingredients. Put the lid on the casserole, bring to the boil and simmer for 45 minutes. Thereafter, remove the lid, eliminate the bouquet garni and cut the cured meats into pieces; drain off any excess liquid and serve these savoury beans and cured meats sprinkled with chopped parsley.

Fresh podded broad
  or haricot beans,
  500 g (1 lb; 5 cups);
  (250 g; 8 oz; 2 1/2
  cups if dried)
Lard (in one piece),
  100 g (4 oz)
Butifarra blanca
  (see p. 22), 150 g (6 oz)
Butifarra negra
  (see p. 22), 100 g (4 oz)
1 onion
1 clove of garlic
Bouquet garni, tied (bay
  leaf, mint, rosemary, thyme)
Aniseed (*matalahúva*) and
  cinnamon (small stick)
Parsley
Dry white wine
Salt and pepper
Cooking fat, 30 g
  (1 1/4 oz; 1 1/2 tbsp)

Serves:	4
Preparation:	15'+5-6h
Cooking:	1h
Difficulty:	● ●
Flavour:	● ● ●
Kcal (per serving):	419
Proteins (per serving):	8
Fats (per serving):	33
Nutritional value:	● ● ●

The suggestions given for Faves al tombet *on page 80 apply here as well: if fresh broad beans are not available other varieties may be used with excellent results.*

PANADONS AMB ESPINACS

Spinach parcels

Fresh spinach,
  500 g (1 lb 2 oz)
Plain flour, 200 g (8 oz;
  1 3/4 cups) (plus extra
  for the pastry board)
1 egg
2 cloves of garlic
Malaga sultanas,
  20 g (3/4 oz; 1 tbsp)
Pine nuts,
  30 g (1 1/4 oz; 1 1/2 tbsp)
Salt
Olive oil

Serves: 4	
Preparation: 30'+30'	
Cooking: 40'	
Difficulty: ●●●	
Flavour: ●●	
Kcal (per serving): 551	
Proteins (per serving): 48	
Fats (per serving): 18	
Nutritional value: ●●●	

1 Put the flour in a mixing bowl with a pinch of salt, add 6 tablespoons of oil then work into a smooth, stiff dough with a hand mixer, adding sufficient cold water to achieve this. Leave the dough to stand for about half an hour. In the meantime, soak the sultanas.

2 Trim the spinach and rinse the leaves repeatedly under cold running water; do not dry the leaves but put them dripping wet into a pot and blanch briefly. Drain, squeeze out all moisture, and then chop them.

3 Peel and finely slice the garlic and sauté it in a pan with 3-4 tablespoons of oil; add the chopped spinach, a pinch of salt, the drained and squeezed sultanas and the pine nuts. Simmer slowly for 7-8 minutes then put this filling to one side.

4 Briefly knead the dough again, adding a little water if necessary to make it pliable. Roll it out fairly thin on a floured pastry board and, using a pastry cutter or a drinking glass, cut out rounds about 10 cm (4 inches) in diameter. Place a ball of filling (about 2.5 cm/1 inch in diameter) in the centre of each round of pastry; fold in two (into a crescent shape), seal the edges, brush the surface of the *panadons* with beaten egg and place on an oven tin lightly greased with oil. Bake in a preheated oven (180°C, 350°F) for 20 minutes. These are delicious served with eggs and *tortillas*.

The monolith by Joan Miró in Plaça El Escorxador, Barcelona.

PATATAS A LA CERDEÑA

Potatoes with lard ▶

| 6 medium-sized potatoes |
| Lard, 100 g (4 oz), |
| in one piece |
| 3 cloves of garlic |
| Salt and pepper |
| Olive oil |

Serves:	4
Preparation:	15'
Cooking:	15'
Difficulty:	●
Flavour:	● ●
Kcal (per serving):	584
Proteins (per serving):	8
Fats (per serving):	36
Nutritional value:	● ● ●

Peel and rinse the potatoes then boil them in slightly salted water; drain (keep the cooking water), slice them then put them into a bowl. Mash them with a potato masher (or food mixer), adding a little of the cooking water to keep them soft. Dice the lard and fry it in a pan with 2 tablespoons of oil; add the finely chopped garlic and sauté slowly. Pour this savoury sauce over the mashed potatoes and season with salt and pepper; mix everything together and serve. This is an excellent accompaniment to red meat dishes.

TORTILLA DE PATATAS

Open omelette with potatoes

| 4 eggs |
| 3-4 potatoes |
| (depending on size) |
| Half an onion |
| Salt |
| Olive oil |

Serves:	4
Preparation:	15'
Cooking:	20'
Difficulty:	● ●
Flavour:	● ●
Kcal (per serving):	453
Proteins (per serving):	16
Fats (per serving):	25
Nutritional value:	● ●

Peel the potatoes, rinse and dry them, then slice them into rounds (not too thick). Put them into a large frying pan with 4-5 tablespoons of oil, trying to keep them from overlapping; cover the pan and fry very gently for about ten minutes, or until they are tender but not too soft. Remove and drain.
Whisk the eggs in a bowl with a pinch of salt, add the drained potatoes and drizzle with raw oil. Leave to stand for 5 minutes.
Peel and finely chop the onion then sauté it for 5-6 minutes in an omelette pan with a further 2-3 tablespoons of oil; add to the egg and potato mixture in the bowl. Grease the pan with a little oil and heat, but do not let the oil smoke; add the mixture and cook over medium heat for 2-3 minutes. Flip the omelette over with the aid of a plate, add a few more drops of oil to the pan if required, and cook the other side. The *tortilla de patatas*, which is the national dish of Spain, is very much appreciated in Catalonia.

TORTILLA
DE TOMATES Y PIMIENTOS

Tomato and sweet pepper open omelette

6 eggs	
3 ripe tomatoes	
4 sweet peppers	
1 aubergine	
Salt	
Olive oil	

Serves: 4	
Preparation: 15'+30'	
Cooking: 25'	
Difficulty: ● ●	
Flavour: ● ● ●	
Kcal (per serving): 410	
Proteins (per serving): 23	
Fats (per serving): 29	
Nutritional value: ● ●	

Rinse the aubergine but do not peel it; cut it into slices and sprinkle coarse salt over them on a plate, pressing them down with a weight for 30 minutes to sweat out the bitter taste. Rinse and dry the slices then cut them into small cubes. Rinse the sweet peppers, remove their stalks, seeds and fibrous parts and cut into strips.

Rinse the tomatoes, remove the seeds, cut into tiny pieces and sauté in a pan with 3-4 tablespoons of oil; add the sweet pepper strips and the aubergine cubes and simmer gently for about ten minutes, stirring frequently. Whisk the eggs in a bowl with a pinch of salt and pour into the pan. Cook the *tortilla* over medium heat, then flip it over and cook the other side. Serve cut into wedges.

Cakes
and
DESSERTS

And, last but not least, exquisite and delicate desserts and pastries reminiscent of times long past, like menjar blanc, and traditional family cooking, like the famous crema catalana: we have selected the top of the tops for you here, recipes that are easy to prepare in your own kitchen for breakfast, snacks or desserts.

6

CREMA CATALANA

Oven-baked custard

8 egg yolks
Castor sugar, 150 g (6 oz)
Demerara sugar, 50 g (2 oz)
Full milk, 1 litre (1 2/3 pt)
Plain flour, 20 g (1/2 oz; 1
   3/4 tbsp)
Piece of lemon rind
Piece of cinnamon

Serves: 6	
Preparation: 20'+2h	
Cooking: 30'	
Difficulty: ● ●	
Kcal (per serving): 404	
Proteins (per serving): 19	
Fats (per serving): 17	
Nutritional value: ● ● ●	

Pour the milk (all except half a glass) into a pan with the lemon rind (without the white pith) and the small piece of cinnamon; bring to the boil then remove immediately from the heat. Cover the pan with a lid and leave to one side for about ten minutes. In the meantime, put the egg yolks into a bowl and beat them to a cream with a hand mixer. Remove the lemon rind and cinnamon stick from the milk, then stir it into the creamed eggs, together with the flour mixed with the remaining half glass of milk. Put the contents of the bowl into a pan and beat continuously over low heat until the custard starts to thicken. Remove from the heat as soon as it starts to boil and pour the custard into individual ovenproof ramekins. Wait until the custard becomes cold then put the ramekins into the fridge for about two hours. A few minutes before the dessert is to be served, switch on the grill of the oven; sprinkle a little demerara sugar over the custard in each ramekin then briefly brown the surface under the grill, making the sugar become toffee.

This last step must be performed as quickly as possibly so that the custard inside remains cold.

GRANIZADO

Lemon water-ice

4 large juicy lemons
  (one of which will decorate
  the glasses)
Castor sugar,
  70 g (2 ¹/₂ oz; 6 tbsp)
Ground ice
  (the equivalent of about
  1.5 litres; 2 ¹/₂ pints
  of water)
Fresh mint (for garnish)

Serves: 4	
Preparation: 30'+1h	
Difficulty: ●	
Kcal (per serving): 69	
Proteins (per serving): 1	
Fats (per serving): 0	
Nutritional value: ● ●	

Well before starting to prepare the water-ice, freeze sufficient ice-cubes or trays of ice to make the amount of ice required for grinding. Rinse all the lemons and peel three of them with a peeler, being careful to remove only the yellow rind and no white pith; put the rind in a large bowl. Cut the peeled lemons in half crosswise and squeeze out the juice into a small bowl; put this to one side.

Pour 1 litre (approx. 2 pints) of boiling water over the lemon rinds and leave to cool completely. When cold, remove the rinds, dissolve the sugar in the aromatic water and add the lemon juice; mix gently and leave to one side for ten minutes. Thereafter, mix again until all the sugar has dissolved. Put this lemonade in the fridge for about one hour, then pass the ice-cubes through the ice-grinder and fill tall drinking glasses almost to the rim with the ground ice. Decorate the glasses with a slice of lemon and a sprig of fresh mint, pour the ice-cold lemonade over the ice and add a drinking straw.

This refreshing *granizado*, a sure remedy against the heat of Summer, can be made with black coffee, or even with Malaga or Jerez wine.

ENSAIMADAS

Sweet twists

1 Dissolve the yeast in 2-3 tablespoons of lukewarm water and blend it into 100 g (4 oz) of flour and a teaspoon of sugar in a bowl. Cover the bowl with a damp kitchen towel and leave to rise in a warm place for one hour. When the dough has risen, blend the remaining flour and sugar in another bowl, together with the pinch of salt and the eggs; knead the mixture with sufficient water to obtain a smooth dough, then incorporate the risen dough.

2 Turn out onto a floured pastryboard and knead at length, gradually adding 2 tablespoons of olive oil, until the dough is smooth and springy. Grease a large bowl, put the dough in it, cover with a kitchen towel and leave to rise again for 2 hours; this time it will double its size. Knead the risen dough for a few minutes, and then divide it into balls weighing about 40 g (1 1/2 oz) each. Roll out one of these balls as thin as possible with a rolling pin, and brush the surface with softened lard.

3 Make it into a ball again, roll out once more and brush the surface as before, then make it into a ball for the third time; at this point, roll it back and forth under the palms of both hands until it becomes about 25 cm (10 inches) long and the thickness of a pencil.

4 Twist this into a tight spiral, press both ends to seal them, then place the twist on a baking tray lined with lightly greased oven paper. Repeat these steps until all the dough has been used up, arranging the twists side by side on the tray but not too near each other. Cover the tray with the same towel as before and leave to stand for about 30 minutes. After this, remove the towel, sprinkle some water over the twists and put the tray in the oven, preheated to 200°C (375°F) to bake for a good ten minutes. Remove the *ensaimadas* from the oven and sift icing sugar over them. These twists belong to Balearic Island traditional fare, but have taken root on the mainland, where they are enjoyed at breakfast time or just as a snack.

Plain flour, 500 g
  (1 lb 2 oz, plus extra
  for flouring
  the pastry-board)
Baker's yeast,
  10 g (^{1}/2 oz)

2 eggs
Castor sugar,
  80 g (3 oz; ^{1}/2 cup)
Icing sugar
Pinch of salt
Lard, 50 g (2 oz)
Olive oil

Serves: 4	Nutritional value: ● ● ●
Preparation: 40'+3h 30'	
Cooking: 20'	
Difficulty: ● ● ●	
Kcal (per serving): 752	
Proteins (per serving): 16	
Fats (per serving): 29	

MENJAR BLANC

Almond blancmange ▶

Almond kernels, 300 g
(12 oz; 1 3/4 cup)
Castor sugar,
150 g (5-6 oz; 1 1/4 cup)
Maize flour,
40 g (1 1/2 oz; 3 tbsp)
Cinnamon (piece)
Strip of lemon rind
Pinch of salt
Olive oil

Serves: 4
Preparation: 20'
Cooking: 35'
Difficulty: ● ● ●
Kcal (per serving): 785
Proteins (per serving): 20
Fats (per serving): 52
Nutritional value: ● ● ●

1 Blanch the almonds for 6-7 minutes in unsalted boiling water; drain and peel then finely grind them (all but 50 g/ 2 oz, to be used later on) and put them into a bowl. Pour 1 litre (a little less than 2 pints) of boiling water over the ground almonds and leave to stand for ten minutes. Filter the liquid through a piece of clean white linen stretched over a pan so that the almond 'milk' will drip through. When only almonds are left in the cloth, gather the corners of the linen together and squeeze out as much 'milk' as possible.

2 Add a piece of cinnamon stick, the lemon rind, 120 g (just over 4 oz/ 8-10 tbsp) of sugar and a pinch of salt to this almond liquid in the pan; bring slowly to the boil, and simmer for ten minutes. Eliminate the cinnamon and lemon rind, and gently stir in the flour mixed with a drop of water. With the heat still at minimum, let the mixture thicken and cook for about fifteen minutes; remove from the stove and pour the mixture into four individual sweet dishes. Allow to cool then put in the fridge for a couple of hours. When it is time to serve the dessert, toast the remaining ground almonds in a small pan with a drizzle of oil and the sugar left over. Take the dishes out of the fridge and sprinkle the toasted almonds over the blancmange.

MEL I MATÓ

Honey and soft cheese

Fresh *queso* or *requesón*
(fresh, soft cheese),
400 g (14 oz)
Honey (acacia, wildflower
or other flavour),
100 g (4 oz; 7 tbsp)

Serves: 4
Preparation: 5'
Difficulty: ●
Kcal (per serving): 417
Proteins (per serving): 27
Fats (per serving): 24
Nutritional value: ● ● ●

Divide the soft but not ice-cold cheese into small serving bowls; add a couple of tablespoons of honey (thin, runny honey is preferable), and serve. This is the simplest of desserts, the most nourishing of snacks, and one of the most enticing titbits. They say in Barcelona, where fresh *queso* is eaten in enormous quantities, that the type from Montserrat is the best quality.

If a hypothetical classification of the most popular sweets and cakes in Catalonia were to be made, then first place would be taken by the Postre de músic, *made with desiccated fruit and sultanas, to be washed down with a glass of* moscatel; *they say it's name arises from the fact that it was usually eaten on Sundays by the musicians playing in public dance halls: the musicians had to play on until late at night and, because they had to have their supper beforehand, they had no time for a dessert – so they put it in their pockets and ate it between one dance and another. Next in the list would be* pressecs amb vi *(quinces with wine),* codonyat *(a thick quince jam called* membrillo *elsewhere in Spain), the* empanadas de calabaza *(sweet pumpkin cakes),* bufats *(almond fritters) and other delights on sale in Catalonia.*